A WONDERLAND OF STONE IN UTAH'S CANYONLANDS NATIONAL PARK.

WINDOW

AMERICAN BALD EAGLE, LIVING SYMBOL OF A NAT

MESA ARCH FRA

ON AMERICA
Discovering Her Natural Beauty

Prepared by the Special Publications Division, National Geographic Society, Washington, D.C.

WINTER GRIPS YOSEMITE VALLEY, MONUMENT TO THE POWER OF GLACIAL ACTIVITY.

GALEN ROWELL/MOUNTAIN LIGHT

WINDOW ON AMERICA
Discovering Her Natural Beauty

Contributing Authors: WILLIAM HOWARTH,
  CHRISTINE ECKSTROM LEE, MARK MILLER,
  THOMAS O'NEILL, BILL RICHARDS,
  JENNIFER C. URQUHART
Contributing Photographers: JOSÉ AZEL,
  RICHARD ALEXANDER COOKE III, DAN DRY,
  DAVID HISER, PHILIP SCHERMEISTER

Published by THE NATIONAL GEOGRAPHIC SOCIETY
  GILBERT M. GROSVENOR, *President
    and Chairman of the Board*
  MELVIN M. PAYNE, *Chairman Emeritus*
  OWEN R. ANDERSON, *Executive Vice President*
  ROBERT L. BREEDEN, *Senior Vice President,
    Publications and Educational Media*

Prepared by THE SPECIAL PUBLICATIONS DIVISION
  DONALD J. CRUMP, *Director*
  PHILIP B. SILCOTT, *Associate Director*
  BONNIE S. LAWRENCE, *Assistant Director*

Staff for this Book
  PAUL MARTIN, *Managing Editor*
  THOMAS B. POWELL III, *Illustrations Editor*
  CINDA ROSE, *Art Director*
  BARBARA A. PAYNE, *Senior Researcher*
  VICTORIA GARRETT CONNORS, *Researcher*
  SUSANNE E. FRÜH, *Research Assistant*
  SEYMOUR L. FISHBEIN, SARA GROSVENOR,
    CHRISTINE ECKSTROM LEE,
    H. ROBERT MORRISON,
    JENNIFER C. URQUHART,
    SUZANNE VENINO, *Picture Legend Writers*
  JOHN D. GARST, JR., D. MARK CARLSON,
    JOSEPH F. OCHLAK, DANIEL J. ORTIZ,
    KEVIN Q. STUEBE, *Map Research and Production*
  HILDEGARD B. GROVES, *Map Artist*
  ARTEMIS S. LAMPATHAKIS, *Illustrations Assistant*
  SEYMOUR L. FISHBEIN, MARY ANN HARRELL,
    Consulting Editors
  JODY BOLT, *Consulting Art Director*

Engraving, Printing, and Product Manufacture
  ROBERT W. MESSER, *Manager*
  GEORGE V. WHITE, *Assistant Manager*
  DAVID V. SHOWERS, *Production Manager*
  GEORGE J. ZELLER, JR., *Production
    Project Manager*
  GREGORY STORER, *Senior Assistant
    Production Manager*
  MARK R. DUNLEVY, *Assistant
    Production Manager*
  TIMOTHY H. EWING, *Production Assistant*
  SHARON K. BERRY, CAROL ROCHELEAU CURTIS,
    MARY ELIZABETH ELLISON, ROSAMUND GARNER,
    BRIDGET A. JOHNSON, SANDRA F. LOTTERMAN,
    ELIZA C. MORTON, CLEO E. PETROFF,
    VIRGINIA A. WILLIAMS, *Staff Assistants*
  GEORGE I. BURNESTON, III, LISA S. JENKINS,
    Indexers

AUTUMN WOODS AND A CLAPBOARD CHAPEL GLOW IN THE BERKSHIRE HILLS OF MASSACHUSETTS.

JONATHAN BLAIR

CONTENTS

FOREWORD

By Donald J. Crump
Director,
Special Publications
Division

DAVID HISER

Photographs are windows of a sort: Through them we view worlds we might otherwise never see—worlds of wonder, distant worlds, worlds of people, places, and things that delight and move us. Framed by the pages of a book such as this one, photographs let us glimpse other lives and other landscapes. For many years, I've been looking through photographic windows, first as a photographer on a small newspaper in Oklahoma, then as a picture editor at the National Geographic Society.

Now, as Director of the Special Publications Division, I review thousands of photographs each year as our editors make selections for our books and magazines. Since many of the previous 83 Special Publications that the Society has produced have dealt with the past, present, or future of the United States, a great number of the photographs I see are of scenes of America's natural wonders. I'm always reminded that, despite centuries of colonization, settlement, growth, and industrialization, much of our country remains breathtakingly beautiful.

In a way, too, photographs show us much more than the world. They also let us look into the soul of the photographer. Because no two photographers see the same scene in the same way, our photographic windows on the world are of endless variety.

For this book, we are pleased to offer the work of a number of especially sensitive photographers. David Muench, long noted for his vistas of the American West, catches the fragile beauty of snow-laden conifers, as well as the imposing visages of Mount Rushmore's presidential figures. David Hiser finds an alpine larch poised with oriental delicacy over a valley in the Bitterroot Range, and José Azel brings us a memorable Massachusetts bullfrog and an elegant maple leaf at rest on a mossy forest floor in Maine.

Dan Dry's portrait of a farmer and his mule is a new look at an old subject, and Steven Fuller captures the familiar cunning of a red fox in an arresting way. Richard Cooke's haunting photograph of Misty Fiords in Alaska brings the book to an appropriate close. There are scenes here from every corner of the country, and the accompanying text makes each chapter memorable. Many of these sites have been familiar to us since childhood—the falls of Yosemite, the rugged mountains of Maine—even though we may never have seen them firsthand.

Over the years as I've looked *through* photographs—treating them as the windows they are—I've often imagined myself a part of the scenes they represent. Viewed in such a way, photographs can reinforce the impulse we all feel to protect our country's natural beauties. In the future, the photographs in this book will become windows in time, allowing our descendants to see us—and the America that we knew.

BESIDE A JUNIPER, VISITORS GAZE ACROSS THE GRAND CANYON.   OPPOSITE: A BLOSSOM SOFTENS A PRICKLY PEAR CACTUS.

CLARET CUP CACTUS FLARES WITH COLOR ON THE RIM OF THE GRAND CANYON.

THE NORTHEAST

In the Midst of a Delicate Garden

Nature's beauty finds subtle expression in the lands of northeastern America, where age has softened the hills and well-trod paths thread the woodlands. Here, a number of small wild places stand protected. In the Mianus River Gorge Preserve, a 457-acre Nature Conservancy property near Bedford, New York, Havemeyer Falls (opposite) cascades over mossy boulders. Though surrounded by homes and towns, the preserve shelters a fragment of the Northeast's primeval wilderness. Its trails offer a place to consider details like a cluster of violets (above), and serene views of the Mianus River (pages 14-15).

THE NORTHEAST

By Christine Eckstrom Lee
Photographs by José Azel

First region of the United States to be fully explored and settled by Europeans, the Northeast covers an area modest in size and scale but rich in its variety of landscapes. Western Maine's mountain-and-lake district and tiny Mianus Gorge both present a glimpse of the forested wilds that shaped pioneer life in the New World. In Massachusetts, Cape Cod and the Berkshire Hills have long inspired artists and writers, especially the 19th-century New England naturalists, who taught an appreciation of the land's beauty that now speaks to all of wild America.

To the early explorers and settlers who sailed to the New World, the first hint of the beauty of northeast America was carried on the wind. Far out at sea they smelled the fragrance of land, of forests and wild strawberries and flowers, "as if we had been in the midst of some delicate garden," one seafarer wrote. The Italian navigator Verrazano, exploring the coast here in 1524, noted that the trees "for a long distance, exhale the sweetest odors," and he detected their scents hundreds of miles from shore.

Since the days of discovery and colonization, we have celebrated the beauty of our New World, fashioning dreams from the lovely fabric of the American landscape. The well-trod and weather-worn lands of northeast America, so long settled and known, hold a collection of scenic places as beloved and familiar as poems memorized in school—places that inspired early artists, writers, and philosophers whose works helped shape America's ideals and destiny. Traveling in the Northeast, where I have both visited and lived, I always feel close to a wellspring of American thought. In the contemplative seasons of autumn and winter I made a pilgrimage around the region's hills, valleys, woodlands, and seacoasts, to places both famed and unsung, to discover the quiet beauty that has stirred imaginations from the time of our ancestors' first breath of the new continent.

When the *Mayflower* Pilgrims sighted land in November 1620, it was not Plymouth but the highlands of Cape Cod. They came ashore and fell to their knees, happy to leave the sea behind. But their pleasure faded when they looked around the Cape—"a hidious and desolate wildernes," in one Pilgrim's words—and they left after a few weeks, bound for Plymouth.

The Pilgrims might have stayed longer had they arrived in summer, when the Cape is balmy and green, the skies are cornflower blue, and the sea sets boats rocking like a baby's cradle. I spent summers on Cape Cod when I was in college, working in seafood restaurants, eating quahogs and scrod, living in an old wooden windmill. I was a Southerner in a place long cherished by New Englanders as a summer retreat, and I was struck that even vacationing families often knew the Cape so well that they had a secret beach plum patch (for making jam) or could show me a little swale in the dunes where a favorite flower grew. I remember the honey-gold light of lingering June evenings and the time at the high tide of summer when the wild roses bloomed, smothering cottages and fences with bright pink blossoms, sweetening the breezes. And I remember longing to roam the Cape in winter, when the wind howls over a land without roses and the powers of nature that make Cape Cod so beautiful are in their season, reshaping the land.

It's hard to walk a straight line down the outer beach of Cape Cod in a February snowstorm, but the incongruous sight of snowdrifts building in the sand dunes and gulls wheeling through swirls of white flakes lured me down to the sea. The snow was blowing in horizontally from the ocean (I had outraced the flakes at just over 30 miles an hour in my

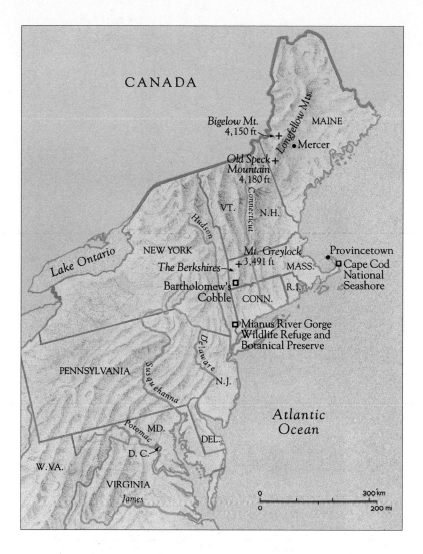

car), so I walked with my face turned inland, to the dunes. Along the northern beaches of the Cape, rolling hills of sand dunes rise to heights of 100 feet above the sea. They are the gift of the glaciers that departed 10,000 years ago, leaving behind the moraine that formed Cape Cod. In summer the dunes look like desert sculptures, immutable as the Pyramids, but in winter waves nibble at their feet and winds sweep great sheets of their sands through the air. With grasses rippling on their crests and pebbles spilling down their steep slopes to the beach, the winter dunes are always in motion. As I trekked down the narrow strand between the boom of the surf and the sifting wall of sand, engulfed in a whirl of big lacy snowflakes, land, sea, and sky all seemed crazily alive, and I felt like a lucky witness to the fury of creation, the only person who stayed to watch a new ice age begin.

I thought of an earlier hiker. In the mid-1800s, the American naturalist Henry David Thoreau made several trips to Cape Cod, walking along the Atlantic beach, watching breakers roll like "a thousand wild horses of Neptune, rushing to the shore, with their white manes streaming far behind." He wrote a book about Cape Cod, describing it as "the bared and bended arm of Massachusetts," and made a prediction unthinkable to the Pilgrims: that the Cape would become a resort. Since 1961, most of Cape Cod's outer arm, from the elbow at Chatham to the fist at Provincetown, has been protected as a national seashore, where anyone may walk in the steps of Thoreau and rediscover the elemental world that inspired him.

Thoreau's prophecy about the popularity of Cape Cod began to come true around the turn of the century, when increasing numbers of summer visitors flocked here. One of America's first art colonies sprang up in Provincetown, and the streets of the small harbor village were suddenly sprinkled with artists seated on sketching stools, painting fishermen and seaside scenes. Authors and playwrights came too, and over the years, Eugene O'Neill, John Dos Passos, Sinclair Lewis, Tennessee Williams, and scores of others have made their homes in Provincetown.

When Napi Van Dereck's family came to Cape Cod in the 1920s, Provincetown was full of Portuguese fishermen and avant-garde artists. "My parents were artists, and they found this a natural place to be," Napi told me. "Artists like to live among themselves, and Provincetown was a wonderful artists' ghetto—it was beautiful, everything was cheap, and they could escape from other people and express themselves freely. Everyone was sparked by the energy of this place."

Napi owns a restaurant and art gallery in Provincetown; he calls his gallery the "Eye of Horus," for the Egyptian god of light, and every time I saw him he wore a beret and a blue jean jacket with a winged eye symbol embroidered on the back. Napi captures the beauty of Cape Cod with his camera on his daily walks through the dunes beyond town. He invited me to join him one afternoon as the falling sun bathed the grasses in rose water light, tinting pockets of snow in the dunes pale pink.

"Cape Cod has a quality of light that you won't find anywhere else in America," Napi said. "It's a marine light, like they have in Holland, reflecting from all the surrounding water, and it makes everything luminous. That's why artists are always attracted to Cape Cod. The eye sees things differently here."

As we followed a winding path through the dunes, Napi entertained me with an offbeat narrative about the Indians and the Pilgrims, his sentences sometimes trailing off when he noticed the changing cast of light. "The Indians used to come up here all the time," he said. "The fish were so abundant that they could be gotten by just pounding on the water, and you could walk along and pick lobsters off the beach. So the Indians would have a grand time here. They'd grow some corn, collect fish, swim—this was partyville. Cape Cod is a great place to spend the summer, and we're not the only ones who have thought that way."

We came to an area known as Pilgrim Springs, where the Pilgrims are said to have first tasted the water of the New World. From the tiny clear pool there I took a drink—cold and sweet—while Napi gazed at the light. The sun set, and the bright color drained from the sky, as if the cold had frozen the gaiety out of the light, chilling it to wan pastels, like the hues of ice. The grasses turned brown, rasping in the wind, and we both fell silent.

Winter beauty on the Cape comes at the price of cold and discomfort, but the rewards are the serene purity of a land stripped of excess. Near Wellfleet, I hiked down the Atlantic White Cedar Swamp Trail; where years ago I had walked the path with groups of summer tourists, I was now the sole explorer of the winter swamp. The trail descends from the dunes into a dank world of tall trees, like the cypress swamps of the South. Strolling through the cedars was like walking among a relaxed and friendly crowd of people. Sinuous ice streams wound around hummocks of green moss where the cedars grew; on the day I visited, the ice was thin and glass-clear, and just under its surface was a perfect collage of the season past and the one to come: red and yellow fall leaves mixed with the seeds of spring, held fast in the glaze of winter.

I suspect that then even Cape Codders, who are accustomed to the sights of their land, still see the particular beauty of their home. I developed a habit of driving from beach to beach, all around the national seashore, to see how the ocean looked in different places on different winter days, and I noticed that when I drove to any beach on a weekday around noon, I would find a row of cars and trucks in the parking lot, all spaced a polite distance apart. There were repair trucks, government cars, and all manner of service vehicles, each pointed to face the sea. Inside each sat someone having a sandwich and soda, spending their lunch hour watching the ocean. When they finished, most looked out to sea just a bit longer before heading back to work. Usually by two o'clock, everyone was gone, and the parking lots would be empty until noon the next day.

I f Cape Cod has an ever changing loveliness, ephemeral as cherry blossoms in an April gust, then the appeal of the Berkshire Hills of western Massachusetts is like that of the West's bristlecone pines—old and sturdy and so everlasting that they are a measure of time itself. The seasons change the garments of the Berkshires—meadows of spring wildflowers, emerald summer greenery, the fire colors of autumn, the fairyland snows—but the hills stand stout as a pursed-lipped old Yankee who doesn't give a hoot about what anyone thinks of him.

I used to go to the Berkshires to hike and ski and explore when I attended college not far from the eastern foothills, and I returned in fall, my favorite time of year there, when the northern air blows in so arctic-clean and clear that every leaf and twig seems in sharper focus. It was the season of color, when from the monochrome mantle of summer green, each tree stands forth as an individual, fresh-dyed in red, yellow, or orange, revealing the separate threads that make the tapestry of the landscape whole. At its peak, fall color never looked like a dying to me, but then one day I would find all the leaves underfoot, curling and brown;

thinking back, I would see the great blazing display as that last brilliant flash of light from a star before it winked out of the cosmos.

As I headed up the valleys of the Housatonic and the Hoosic, the two main watercourses of the Berkshires, the soft profile of hills filled me with the feeling of familiarity that makes precise memories return. During college, I sometimes walked in these woods to think, hoping that some notion of what Melville really meant would come to me in the hills he knew, or that a stray thought of Hawthorne's would be whispered to me in the hush of the forest.

Melville had a home in the Berkshires, as did Hawthorne, Jonathan Edwards, Oliver Wendell Holmes, William Cullen Bryant, and Edith Wharton; Harriet Beecher Stowe, Longfellow, James Russell Lowell, and the ever wandering Thoreau came here, too. I remember that it once seemed to me that all great dead American writers were New Englanders, and that most of them (especially the ones that were topics of English course essays) had lived in the Berkshires.

Even a century ago, people felt the need to escape from the bustle of the city to the peace and solitude of the countryside. But not all of the illustrious authors always found the Berkshires to their liking: Hawthorne wrote *The House of the Seven Gables* at his home in Lenox and rhapsodized about the beauty of the hills in other books—and then railed against the changeable weather in his notes: "I detest it! I detest it!! I detest it!!! I hate Berkshire with my whole soul, and would joyfully see its mountains laid flat." Longfellow, although he returned often to the Berkshires, wrote in his journal, "I find it quite impossible to write in the country, the influences are soothing and slumberous." He seems to have spent his time there resting: Two days later he noted, "The capacity of the human frame for sleep in the summer is very great. . . ."

Melville, however, always seemed to find inspiration in the Berkshires. He lived there for 13 years, writing *Moby-Dick, The Piazza Tales,* and other books at Arrowhead, his home just outside Pittsfield. He built the piazza of his *Tales* along the north side of his home, so that it faced Mount Greylock, the highest peak in the Berkshire region. In the landlocked hills he found images of the sea. From his piazza, he wrote, ". . . long ground-swells roll the slanting grain . . . and the blown down of dandelions is wafted like the spray, and the purple of the mountains is just the purple of the billows . . . the vastness and the lonesomeness are so oceanic, and the silence and the sameness, too, that the first peep of a strange house, rising beyond the trees, is for all the world like spying, on the Barbary coast, an unknown sail."

He once described his house as a ship at sea, and like *Moby-Dick*'s Captain Ahab aboard the *Pequod,* Melville walked his piazza, even in bitterest winter, "for then, once more, with frosted beard, I pace the sleety deck, weathering Cape Horn."

A fresh snowfall had just blanketed the Berkshires when I visited Melville's home. It was now midwinter, and no footprints but mine marked the snows around Arrowhead. *(Continued on page 29)*

Litter of fallen leaves marks the end of the season of color in the Berkshire Hills of western Massachusetts. Herman Melville wrote of these hills in autumn, "I tell you that sunrises and sunsets grow side by side in these woods and momentarily moult in the falling leaves." Melville moved to the Berkshires in 1850, where, though strapped for money and burdened by farm life, he poured out 5,000 words a day, crafting the immortal Moby-Dick.

A foot trail, walked at a leisurely pace, rewards the patient observer with a peek at the small worlds of life tucked in the Berkshire woodlands. Down at pond level, a bullfrog lingers for a look at who's watching. A cecropia caterpillar (opposite, left) inches its many-legged way along a stem; an interrupted fern and a parasol mushroom (left) form an artful composition on a decaying log.

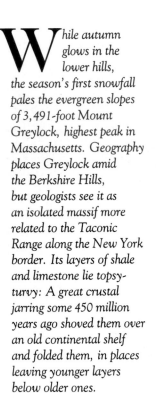

While autumn glows in the lower hills, the season's first snowfall pales the evergreen slopes of 3,491-foot Mount Greylock, highest peak in Massachusetts. Geography places Greylock amid the Berkshire Hills, but geologists see it as an isolated massif more related to the Taconic Range along the New York border. Its layers of shale and limestone lie topsy-turvy: A great crustal jarring some 450 million years ago shoved them over an old continental shelf and folded them, in places leaving younger layers below older ones.

S till life of the changing seasons: A red maple leaf, bright emblem of autumn in the Northeast, rests on a carpet of summer-green moss on a forest floor in western Maine, where long, bitter winters make the brief months of blossoms, greenery, and color all the sweeter.

Melville's beloved piazza had been long ago removed, but the view to the heights of Greylock was unchanged—an open vista of rolling blue hills with Greylock's crown shining white with snow. Looking at the seascape of hills every day, Melville would have noticed a feature of the winter skyline that I saw for the first time with a thrill: The summits of Greylock and a nearby peak look like the head and tail of a great white whale, breaching the blue waves of the Berkshires.

In *Moby-Dick,* Melville depicted the whale's hump as a monadnock, a mountain that stands alone. This unusual word is one of several New Englanders use for their ancient landforms. The Berkshires abound with knolls and cobbles—small nubs of hills that have resisted some 450 million years of tectonic heavings and erosion. Geologists say that once the Berkshires may have soared as high as the Himalayas; now the region's tallest mountain rises less than 3,500 feet. But like New England itself, the Berkshires are settled down, broken in, and not too flashy, just the way the people like them.

I was intrigued by the homey quaintness of the name Bartholomew's Cobble, a dot on the map in the southern Berkshires, near the Connecticut border. Owned by the Trustees of Reservations, a private conservation group, Bartholomew's Cobble is a nature preserve covering a little less than 300 acres, and it actually contains two cobbles.

Standing side by side along an oxbow in the Housatonic, the twin cobbles rise about a hundred feet above the river. Covered with hemlocks, pines, and hardwoods, they are difficult to discern from certain angles. But under the shady boughs lies a remarkable rock garden world that supports some 800 species of plants, including perhaps more varieties of fern than are found anywhere else in the continental United States. Such a site, small but rich in subtle wonder, is just the sort of place that New Englanders so fondly protect.

Although it was off-season for the Cobble, resident naturalist Douglas Cross offered to guide me along one of its trails. "This is not the best time of year for the ferns," he said, "but we'll see what winter survivors are here." The first survivors greeted us at the trailhead. Dozens of Christmas ball-size chickadees decorated the bare branches of a tree, waiting for someone to open the glass jar of sunflower seeds resting on a signboard by the path. "The Indians here referred to these as their best-loved birds," Doug said, "because they stuck around all winter long. They were so small and yet so brave." We fed them from our hands (their tiny feet tickle when they wrap around a finger), and Doug filled his pockets with seeds to dole out to them as we walked the trail.

Under the evergreens, the Cobble was dark and frosty and full of tall boulders, some with sizable trees growing up from their ledges, the roots gripping the rock walls. Doug pointed to a boulder. "There are 80 different species of plants on that one rock," he said. "Most of the rock here is marble with quartzite mixed in. The quartzite resists weathering and makes the rock strong. That's why the Cobble stands proud, like an island. And the soil is rich in lime, which the ferns love. People come

Bright-eyed note of winter cheer, a black-capped chickadee perches on a branch empty of leaves in a Maine forest. Maine's extensive timberlands—besides providing wildlife habitat—have long played a major role in the state's economy. Lands logged to stubble at the turn of the century have grown back, with many scenic areas now set aside as parks.

from all over to see the ferns and wildflowers. A moss specialist once identified a species never before reported in the United States. It's a moss that's usually a resident of the Middle East, and he found it growing on an old apple tree here on the Cobble."

The chickadees followed us down the trail, flitting from tree to tree. "The Housatonic River is a flyway, and we've had more than 240 species of birds reported here," Doug said. A woodpecker tapped on a tree. "The pileated woodpecker is making a comeback in this area, and all over New England, because a lot of old farm fields are reverting to woodlands," he explained. "Around the turn of the century, this area was much more open. Cows grazed on the Cobble. It was the artists who came here to paint the river and the early naturalist-explorers in the region who first realized that this was a pretty special spot, geologically and botanically. It's a real gem," he added, "and I think that in New England, people put a lot of effort into protecting little nooks like this, because when they're gone, they're gone. If someone had built a house up here, that might well have been the end of the Cobble."

The ice boomed on the Housatonic. "There's a strong sense of history in New England, and a powerful conservation ethic," Doug said. "Even though the places we protect may be small, they're significant. Our land is human-size. Our mountains are not threatening or awesome; they look like they've been lived in—and they have. If you walk up in the mountains, you'll find old roads, stone walls, cemeteries—in the middle of the forest. That's what I love about this region. You can be hiking in the woods, with the feeling that no one has ever been there before, and suddenly you'll come to a place where someone lived long ago. There's the well, and there's the lilac bush that was by the front door. It's a piece of history, someone's life. There's so much here, and so much more to discover than first meets the eye."

We rounded a bend to finish the circular trail around the Cobble, and Doug pointed to the snow on the ground. "Wing marks," he said. "From the chickadees." Delicately printed in the snow were the shapes of wing feathers, where the chickadees had landed for a moment, then taken off to fly ahead of us. I looked up and they were back in the tree at the trailhead, waiting by the jar of sunflower seeds.

Whether or not everyone will admit it, winter is always lurking somewhere in the back of every New Englander's mind, and it makes the pleasures of other seasons all the sweeter. Evidence of winter can be detected year-round: the wooden boards to shutter the summer cottage, stashed behind the shed; the piles of firewood that grow larger as autumn progresses; the tall poles staked along mountain roads to measure the depth of snow. Nowhere does the longest season of New England assert itself with more force than in Maine. In the rugged mountain-and-lake country of western Maine, a sparsely settled region brooding with dark forests, winter can be as nasty as it is beautiful—with the land resplendent in ermine coats of snow. People there often love the challenge of the cold, and the worse it gets, the more they like it.

I knew that I had been affected by the Maine winter spirit when I opened the curtains to a snowstorm one morning and felt delighted, because I was watching the raw material, falling from the sky, for the shelter I would sleep in that night. I was heading into the teeth of winter, Maine style, going backpack-cross-country-ski-snow-cave camping near the base of the Bigelows, a wilderness range with 4,000-foot peaks just east of the small town of Stratton. The Bigelows have a rough-born loveliness, and I wanted to step beyond a car window view of winter in Maine and wake up to the mountains, open-air.

My companion-guides were well versed in the Maine wilds: Chuck Dunn, who owns a rafting company in Kingfield and works as a ski patroller; Cathy McKinnon, who used to work for L. L. Bean and knew the right clothes to wear; and Joshua Cook, a medical student from Biddeford, who knew how to build the snow cave. My only concern for the much-promised warmth of the snow cave came from learning that Joshua enjoyed kayaking in the ocean off Maine—in January.

Laden with packs, we skied several miles down an old logging road, through temple columns of pines, blinking wet snowflakes from our eyes, to the shore of Flagstaff Lake, where the Bigelows rose somewhere above us, invisible in the snow clouds. Chuck and Joshua spent the afternoon heaping snow into a broad ten-foot-tall mound, then hollowing out the inside. Cathy and I set up a kitchen camp and heated a rich moose stew prepared for us by Dan Davis, owner and chef of a country inn in Kingfield, who handed us the stew with quips about the last supper—and said, when invited to join us, "No way."

It was still snowing heavily by dusk, and the boughs of the evergreens drooped to the ground under their burden of snow. I walked a short distance out on the lake and, turning in a slow circle, I could see absolutely nothing but the snow before my eyes. No horizon separated land from sky. I had no shadow—and no depth perception, only the sensation that I was standing on a cloud, and that with one step I would fall into nothingness. It was a whiteout, a phenomenon that has always confused explorers of snowbound lands. There was no wind, no voices from camp, and I was muffled in such complete stillness that I could hear the snow fall. I listened for a while, in a winter bell jar, savoring the strange silence of the northland that makes people thinkers or dreamers or madmen—or storytellers.

The snow stopped before midnight, and the clouds sailed away, unveiling a full moon and a bowl of stars. The snow cave beckoned. We had been letting it "set": During the hollowing phase, Joshua explained, his body heat melted a thin layer of the inside walls, and we needed to let it refreeze. To my pleasure, the snow cave was warm (we even had candles on snow shelves inside), and for all my fears of being cold, it was, ironically, a bit too warm: I was awakened early, not by sunrise, but by a fallen chunk of the snow cave ceiling. Joshua, true to his winter-kayaking spirit, had spent most of the night skiing in the moonlight. "It was beautiful," he told us. "The moon was so bright that the trees cast shadows on the snow. I was too exhilarated to go to sleep."

Against an ocean-blue sky, the Bigelows seemed as noble as the Tetons, a zigzag ridgeline of peaks capped with snow, like a child's drawing of mountains. We skied around the lake all afternoon, and as we headed back down the old logging road at dusk, Chuck assessed the snow with an eye to spring rafting. "This part of Maine has one of the greatest water resources in the country," he said. "It's pure and clean and there are more white-water rivers here that may have never been run than anywhere else in the East. In the spring, when they release the water from this lake into the Dead River, the same snow that provided our shelter will give us our white-water thrills."

Around the turn of the century, lumbermen saw a more utilitarian beauty in Maine's water resources when they clear-cut much of the sea of trees that covered the state and floated the logs down the frothy rivers. Of the forested hills in the region around Kingfield, Dan Davis told me, "Eighty years ago, a lot of this land was bald. I've seen old pictures of lumbermen standing on clear-cut land with a look on their faces of stunned exhaustion—like the faces of sod-house pioneers in Kansas."

In Maine, and all around New England, forests have grown up again, both on land once cut over by timber companies and in places where people abandoned their farms, many for the lure of richer westward lands. There were also those, especially after World War II, who simply left the rigors of life in rural New England for jobs in cities or warmer climes, and their lands, too, have reverted to forest. All across New England, I saw, overgrown in the woods, beautiful stone walls—someone's years of labor to build a boundary against the wilds, where, for whatever reason, the wilds had triumphed.

A new influx of settlers came to New England at the crest of the back-to-the-land movement of the late sixties and early seventies in search of a fresh inspiration from the land, another way of life in America. Some came with a reverence for the early New England naturalists, who taught us to appreciate the marvels and details of the world we see every day, to understand what Thoreau meant when he wrote in *Walden*, "I have travelled a good deal in Concord"—his own backyard. Not everyone stayed, but near Mercer, Maine, I met a man who did. In keeping with the New England literary tradition that has not varied so much as her forests, Baron Wormser is a poet, and, like Thoreau's, his vision is rooted in the land where he has chosen to live, in his new backyard.

Baron, his wife Janet, and their two children live in the woods, in a lovely log and shingle home they helped to build, forsaking electricity and telephones for the comforts of a wood stove, kerosene lamps, and walls full of books. They cut their own wood, grow their own food (Janet also dabbles in dahlias), and Baron works as a librarian.

"We wanted to live in the country," he told me. "We like solitude.

When you look at the map, it's astonishing how few people there are between here and Canada. It was all inhabited once, and part of the appeal here is the bittersweet quality of a landscape of abandonment. It has a hard beauty; it's not a glamorous place—it's real. You're really off on your own. You're responsible for yourself, in all kinds of ways. That's why a lot of people moved up here—to live their own lives."

Baron grew up in Baltimore, and he and Janet lived briefly in California, but didn't like it. "We're real Easterners," he said. "We like the seasons. The weather is a powerful presence in your life here. There's this more or less endless winter. That does set the tone; you have to stay ahead of winter—the wood, the food have to be dealt with in summer. In January, when it's so elemental, you're aware of the cosmic indifference of nature. I think that seeps into the whole character of this place. There are comic aspects too: We always joke about the people who relish adversity—and are dismayed when nature goes well—because it's so much of the identity of living up here."

It grew dark, and Janet lit lamps around the room. "For myself," Baron said, "I feel very much a part of the New England literary tradition. Thoreau, Hawthorne, Emerson—they're real presences to me. Living here, I understand the sort of life they were concerned with living. Any artist is trying to exert control over a medium. You want every rhythm to be right, and you want to live your life that way too. And this place has a history. If you live here, you feel connected to something that goes beyond the present moment or the present literary scene, because certain things don't change. January doesn't change. It was the same in 1850 and 1750.

"New England was settled by people who revered the word," he continued. "And Maine still has an enormous readership. One night at the local grange, a friend of ours brought in one of my poems, and they read it and talked about it. I like that," he said. In one of his poems, "Cord of Birch," Baron wonders about the firewood he has cut in the spring, worrying until winter whether it will burn well:

> By New Year's the snow was over two feet deep;
> Load by load my dilemma was taken away,
> And often I stopped to stare on my way
> Back from the shed at the smoke the fire had freed
> And let myself be gratified by the wisdom of need.

In spite of the efforts of farmers and lumbermen and home builders, there are still places in the Northeast that were too tough to clear, and that still look as they did three and a half centuries ago when the *Mayflower* Pilgrims reached Cape Cod. Curiously, one such wild beauty spot, Mianus River Gorge, lies just beyond the madding crowds of New York City, near Bedford, close to the Connecticut line. Set aside in 1955, the gorge was the first project of the Nature Conservancy, a conservation group that over the years has helped save

Icy close-up of a snow-caked pine bough captures the penetrating cold, and the delicate beauty, of Maine's frozen time of year. "In January, when it's so elemental, you're aware of the cosmic indifference of nature," says Maine poet Baron Wormser. "Winter is the closest thing to eternity you're going to experience."

more than two and a half million acres of critical natural habitats.

The preserve parallels the steep banks of the Mianus River, which carves a cascading path through 150-foot-high rocky hills. On a sunny winter day, I walked the nature trail along the gorge with Anne French, executive director of the volunteer committee that manages the property, and I remarked to her that I had once lived in New Canaan, not eight miles away, but that I had never heard of the gorge. "Most people who live in this area haven't been here," she said. "And it's a good thing—if everyone came, the gorge would be in danger of being *loved* to death."

The preserve is literally Anne's home; she grew up on 40 acres her family has donated to the Mianus Gorge lands. "This preserve represents a private, local conservation effort," she explained. "In 1950 a woman named Gloria Hollister Anable was riding horseback up the valley with her husband and they came to this extraordinary stretch of river. She was struck by the majesty of the hemlocks and the peace of it all and how untouched it was. In 1954, Mrs. Anable discovered that 60 acres were about to be sold to a developer. She and her friends had one week to collect a down payment. They went door to door to raise the money—and they succeeded," Anne said. "Now we have 457 acres—almost all of it by private gift. In 1964, we were declared the first national natural landmark. Stewart Udall himself came up here. I like to think, too, that we're the jewel in the crown of the Nature Conservancy."

We trudged through deep snow along the trail to a grove of hemlocks as high as the walls of the gorge—a virgin stand. "These trees were saplings about the time that the Pilgrims were settling Plymouth," Anne said. "You don't see many trees like these in this part of the country. I remember visiting the redwood forest out West; when we walked in, my daughter glanced up and said, 'Looks like home.' When you see these hemlocks, it helps you to understand what the first settlers had to contend with when they were given a grant of land in the New World."

We hiked down a steep slope, over snowy boulders, to a bubbling pool at the base of a waterfall. "I love this place," Anne said. "When I was a girl, I knew every inch of this land. It was idyllic, totally dark. I imagined little elves and nymphs sitting on the edge of the pool. To me, it was mystery. I felt something when I was down here, especially in late summer evenings, and some of my friends did, too. There are certain places where you sense something mystical—and this is one. I'm sure this place was sacred to the Indians. I can feel it.

"That's why I feel so strongly today about the land my family has given to the preserve. I want my great-great-grandchildren to come here too, to walk and dream."

We retraced our steps, up the boulders and through the hemlocks. "Generations from now, people will be able to come here and still see what our forefathers saw," she said. "It's an awe-inspiring thought." The breeze shook snow from the hemlocks and filled the air with the aroma of evergreens. "Is that the scent of hemlocks?" I asked Anne. "I'm not sure," she said. "To me it just smells like home."

Maine's sea of rugged hills for a backdrop, wilderness guide Joe
Lentini snowshoes across a high plateau outside Grafton Notch
State Park near the New Hampshire border. The white summit
of Old Speck rises 4,180 feet in the near distance. John Matyas (opposite), a
member of the daylong outing, takes a gentle tumble into a snowbank. At far
right, Lentini trudges up a slope near the open plateau—where the trees are
stunted, the winds bone-chilling, and the vistas splendid.

Flashing beam of Eastham's Nauset lighthouse warns mariners of their approach to Cape Cod, Massachusetts, where the Mayflower Pilgrims first landed in November 1620. In his classic book, The Outermost House, Henry Beston described the Nauset light at night, "now as a star of light which waxes and wanes three mathematic times, now as a lovely pale flare of light behind the rounded summits of the dunes."

THE SOUTHEAST
History's Verdant Treasurelands

Lush lands of the Southeast reflect a rich combination of history and natural
    marvels. Through the Cumberland Gap to "Caintuck" strode Daniel
    Boone, followed by land-hungry settlers. The dark woodlands there still
    beckon; the reward today may be the sight of a great rhododendron in
bloom (above). On these blossoms rests a spicebush swallowtail. Bald cypress trees
guard the murky water of Reelfoot Lake in northwest Tennessee (opposite), where
abundant fish draw spring anglers. Winter at Reelfoot yields other attractions.
The ten-mile-long lake lies on the migration route of Canada geese (pages 46-47).

THE SOUTHEAST

By Thomas O'Neill
Photographs by Dan Dry

Southern treasurelands: Kentucky's Cumberland Gap National Historical Park and Daniel Boone National Forest guard lands the pioneers wrested from the Cherokee and Shawnee. In northwest Georgia, 2,000-foot-deep Cloudland Canyon remains largely untouched by man. Formed by earthquakes, Reelfoot Lake abounds in plants and animals. Florida's Jupiter Island harbors a major nesting area for endangered sea turtles, and a beach— Blowing Rocks—where the surf can put on geyser-like displays.

A pocketful of cowries, a few lightning whelks, and a sunray venus or two make for an exalted day's shelling on Jupiter Island. Yet compared with what the sea has pitched up in the past onto this 16-mile-long barrier island off Florida's southeast coast, this haul can seem . . . well, rather humdrum. Burlap sacks of Prohibition-era liquor, a cargo of tires for Model T Fords, barrels of flour, crates of fruit—all have washed ashore, all from shipwrecks. The tides here have delivered up everything from Spanish gold pieces to bales of marijuana. On warm spring and summer nights the sea is especially generous. It is then that a beachcomber on Jupiter Island may be treated to a glimpse of one of the sea's rarer creatures.

A stampede of clouds raced across the midnight sky as Stuart Marcus, assistant manager of the Hobe Sound National Wildlife Refuge, led me down a pitch-black beach on the island's northern end. We swept the sand with our flashlight beams as we moved slowly aboard a vehicle that was half dune buggy, half motorcycle. The Atlantic surf boomed dully in our ears. Suddenly Stuart's beam froze, illuminating what looked like the track of a bulldozer. His light climbed the beach to the high-tide line of strewn seaweed, stopping on a dark shape. "There's your sea turtle," Stuart announced. It was a loggerhead. We came closer and saw its broad, thick head and craggy snout jutting from a shell that was at least three feet long and marked with a constellation of white barnacles. Our voices and lights didn't seem to bother the turtle at this point: She had already embarked on her single-minded task of depositing shiny white eggs into a cavity she had dug with her back flippers.

The loggerhead is one of three species of marine turtles that, between April and September, emerge from the sea at night and crawl up Jupiter Island beaches to lay their eggs. The other two species are the green and the leatherback. The populations of all three species have declined markedly worldwide because of predators and other pressures, with the green and leatherback currently on the endangered species list. The loggerhead is by far the most common of the sea turtles to visit Jupiter Island, its nests numbering more than 2,500, making the island one of the world's major nesting areas for this species.

As the night deepened, Stuart and I stood on the deserted beach watching the loggerhead fulfill her biological mission. Though the refuge is closed to visitors from sundown to sunrise, I was getting a special glimpse of this rare turtle. After dropping her eggs, the loggerhead, with much wheezing and groaning, filled the hole with swipes of her flippers, and then flattened the area with a slow turning of her body before dragging herself back to the sea. "This is all very strenuous for her," Stuart said sympathetically. "She's streamlined for water. Laying eggs is the only time in her whole life cycle that she will come on land."

With the hundreds of miles of beachfront along the country's southeastern coast, what, I wondered the next day, attracts so many oceangoing turtles to tiny Jupiter Island? My eyes supplied the answer. In the refuge and in other protected areas, I would often simply stand in

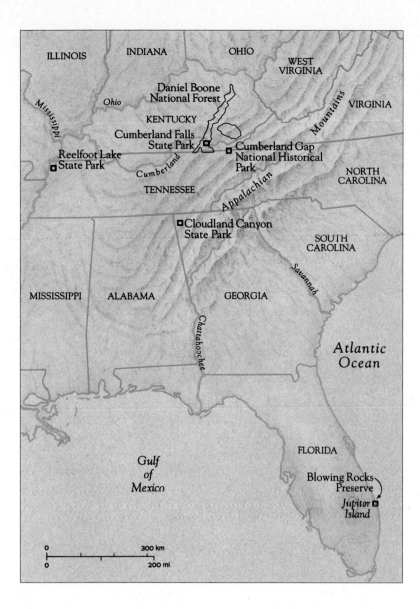

the surf, gazing in all directions to take stock of my surroundings. Was there a golf course ribboning the coastline, a condominium etched on the horizon? Was there a bar nearby, a marina, a mansion hidden by a hedge? There were none of these in sight. What I saw was the splendor of a wild beach, that Florida rarity, a stage upon which the pageant of sea meeting land could be witnessed without distraction.

In all, nearly eight miles of seashore—half of Jupiter Island's total coastline—is protected in its undeveloped state, meaning it goes by its proper name of coastal strand rather than as "oceanfront property." I had discovered Jupiter Island as part of an assignment to find a few of the South's less-celebrated scenic treasures. Wild pockets of the darkly forested Cumberland Plateau, whose lush vegetation hides a rich tale of history and an array of unexpected landforms, and earthquake-created

49

Reelfoot Lake in western Tennessee would also star on my agenda.

Jupiter Island owes its state of grace primarily to the farsightedness of its leading family. In the 1930s, Joseph V. Reed, a theatrical producer, bought a sizable portion of the island, which at the time was sparsely populated by people and densely covered by mangroves and thickets of wild lime, coco plum, and gumbo limbo. The island soon attracted a coterie of wealthy residents. By the 1960s, in the face of a development boom as inexorable as the tides, the Reed family began earmarking land to be set aside as wilderness sanctuaries. From the donations of the family and their friends came today's Hobe Sound National Wildlife Refuge.

"We look different because my father did not care to make money off Jupiter Island." I was speaking with Nathaniel Reed, son of the island's deceased patriarch, and president of the Hobe Sound Company, the family's landholding concern. A dedicated conservationist in his own right, Nathaniel presently sits as a high-ranking officer of the National Audubon Society. In his cool, paneled office he paid homage to his father: "In the sixties, when I was considering building a golf course on the island's north end, my father mentioned that he had had such enjoyable times walking that beach. 'Don't develop it,' he said. 'I want at least one wild beach left in Florida.' "

Of all the priceless wild beaches on Jupiter Island, the one called Blowing Rocks most captured my loyalty. Centerpiece of a 113-acre tract of seashore ecosystems owned by the Nature Conservancy, Blowing Rocks Beach on the island's southern half looks like no typical Florida sunbathing strand. More than 120 plant species flourish here. A dune line bristles with Spanish bayonet, a desert plant comfortably at home in the salt spray and muggy heat. At the water's edge stands a mile-long brow of pitted and gnarled limestone that rises more than six feet high, standing in dramatic contrast to the sandy beach on either side of it. These are the blowing rocks. The unusual ledge was formed from the remains of coral, shellfish, and other marine life that had accumulated on a low spot on a sandbar a hundred thousand years ago.

During my first visit in April, the ocean was too flat to gush up through the myriad of fissures and holes in the rocks. Come back when there are small craft warnings, I was told. I returned in June just as a tropical depression was roiling the Atlantic. By high tide in the late afternoon the rocks had exploded. Geyser-like eruptions of water shot a hundred feet high in a kind of stutter step down the entire mile of rock. Rainbows streaked through the spray; plumes and fountains blossomed with each onset of wave; and the whole scene was as rousing as the most breathtaking of fireworks displays.

The unblemished scenery of Jupiter Island provides a way of coming closer to the past—of being able to imagine, for instance, how the Florida coast must have appeared to Spanish explorers in the 16th century. Similarly, the entrancing vistas of the Cumberland Plateau of eastern Kentucky give a glimpse of another time in our nation's history. I was glorying in a late spring afternoon atop the plateau—the western edge of the Appalachian Mountains—as I hiked a ridgeline near where the boundaries of Kentucky, Tennessee, and Virginia meet. Below me, out of sight, ran a cleft through the mountain wall, an opening known as the Cumberland Gap. I was at the moment heeding an exhibition of swallowtail butterflies, a half dozen or so swooping about like kites in the wind, their blue-tinged wings shining like satin in the shafts of light. Lizards refused to budge from their plots of sunlit rock in the dim, enveloping forest of hemlock, hickory, and maple. Hidden above me warblers called in the treetops, while alongside the trail delicate blossoms of mountain laurel splashed the underbrush with pink and white, lending the thick woods the elegance of an English garden.

Two hundred years earlier, shortly after America's revolutionaries had sent their British rulers packing, great numbers of pioneers moved on foot and horseback through Cumberland Gap, arduously making their way to the spacious land of "Caintuck." Cumberland Gap—its discovery credited in 1750 to Virginia surveyor Thomas Walker—permitted land-hungry Americans to breach at last the East's great mountain barrier. Unsuitable for wagons, the rough-hewn path the emigrants followed had been blazed in 1775 by a team of 30 axmen led by a restless farmer from North Carolina named Daniel Boone. More than 300,000 settlers would end up filing across the Kentucky mountains on the Wilderness Trail between 1775 and 1800. But did those courageous families and bold adventurers appreciate the scenic wilderness they had entered?

"The aspect of these cliffs is so wild and horrid that it is impossible to behold them without terror." Thus Daniel Boone described the approach to the gap. "What a road we have passed!" wrote Bishop Francis Asbury, an early Methodist circuit rider. "Certainly the worst on the whole continent. . . . Our way is over mountains, steep hills, deep rivers, and muddy creeks; a thick growth of reeds for miles together; and no inhabitants but wild beasts and savage men." "Killed a fine bear" amounted to an oration of praise from the early travelers.

"The mountains were a dangerous place, where you were exposed," explained Daniel A. Brown, historian at the Cumberland Gap National Historical Park. "On the other side of the gap you entered hostile territory. It must have been an awesome experience crossing the gap in those days, but not in terms of beauty. We look at the landscape differently than the pioneers did. To them the woods were the enemy."

What made the Kentucky wilderness especially dreadful in the minds of the pioneers was the constant threat of Indian attack. Following the approximate route of the Wilderness Road—north from Cumberland Gap through today's towns of Pineville, Flat Lick, and London, and over the ridge into Crab Orchard—I came across a telling reminder of the storied emigration trail. It was a small burial plot filled with coarse stones at the Levi Jackson Wilderness Road State Park.

On this spot on October 3, 1786, more than 20 pioneers, members of the McNitt party, were slain by a band of Indians. The settlers had unwittingly invaded the traditional hunting grounds of the Cherokee and Shawnee, who had their own notions of freedom and prosperity to protect. In 1784 alone, more than a hundred travelers were killed on the trail by Indians. The resistance lasted until 1796, when a series of strikes by pioneer militia finally drove the Indians from the Wilderness Road.

The experience of penetrating a dense, engulfing woods is still a potent one in the Kentucky mountains. Outside the town of Stanton, near where Daniel Boone is said to have sighted the "promised land" of Caintuck, I arranged a hike into Tight Hollow, one of the few remaining tracts of primeval forest left in eastern Kentucky. I was joined by Al Cornett, a landscape painter who had quit an ulcer-producing corporate job in Lexington ten years before, and by Dell Sasser, a bearded biology instructor at Lees College in Jackson, Kentucky.

Hiking into the hollow, we entered jungle-like woods. Tree trunks were black with moisture; tangles of rhododendrons rose ten feet high—the "laurel hells" of the pioneer accounts; and the umbrella trees, or big leaf magnolias, shut out the light. Orange salamanders clung to the mossy cliff walls, and overhead a red-eyed vireo chattered. "That's called the preacher bird," Dell said, "because it never stops talking." Wiping spiderwebs from our faces, we were soon dwarfed by colossal tulip poplars and hemlocks, their trunks as massive as Roman columns.

Dell, who does wildflower paintings, stopped to admire the blossoms of a mountain laurel, marveling that he could never capture their essential pinkness. Stepping over a fallen tree, Al discovered a fungus as large as his own artist's palette. We stopped in front of a small rock shelter and doused our faces with water spilling down from the cliff ledge. From boulder thrones we looked out over the green world that enclosed us and declared that, to us, these woods were a friend.

I often imagined how a party of weary pioneers would have regarded Cumberland Falls had they strayed west from the Gap and suddenly come upon it. Approaching the broad tumult of water plunging 65 feet, they probably would have groaned in dismay that such an obstacle had been placed in their path. As for me, a traveler with the luxury of contemplating, not battling, the wilderness, I found myself gazing raptly at the falls, impressed that such a cataract should exist in the eastern mountains. The falls were flush from several days' rainfall, and as the surging, mud-stained Cumberland River poured over the 125-foot-wide ledge in a dizzying surrender to gravity, the forest itself seemed to roar, as if in defiant pride of keeping its wildness and its capacity to unnerve.

If Cumberland Falls, by its size and spectacle, seems unusual in its Appalachian setting, then the land features of the Red River Gorge, 80 miles to the northeast, must rate as positively exotic. In an area of 30 square miles, some 100 natural sandstone arches have been found, the greatest concentration on the continent except for the formations of the Colorado Plateau region of Utah. (Continued on page 58)

Heir to the expertise of five generations, Julie Oliver, age 12, plays for her grandfather Bud Adkins in New Salem, Georgia. Julie performs with the Adkins Family Band as its only female fiddler. A few miles north of New Salem, Daniel Creek plummets 90 feet over limestone bluffs (pages 54-55). Showy rhododendron blooms brighten the dark forest. The waterfall flows inside Cloudland Canyon, which often lies blanketed by clouds, especially in winter.

And these Kentucky arches are not miniatures, either. Reaching Gray's Arch on a trail leading from deep forest to a precipitous ridgeline, I saw a rock span in whose opening a townhouse could fit.

Many of the large arches are on the rim of the gorge. Below the rim I discovered surprises as well. During Memorial Day weekend I went hiking with Don Fig, a ranger at the Daniel Boone National Forest, and Dr. Fred Coy, an orthopedic surgeon from Louisville. Don briskly led the way, pointing out various spots where he had roped himself down sheer cliffs to rescue careless campers and hikers. In his familiarity with the area and with his air of imperturbable calm, Don seemed a throwback to the able woodsmen of Daniel Boone's age. "You could put me anywhere in here blindfolded and within 15 minutes I'd be oriented and on my way out," he told me matter-of-factly as we stood gazing out over the 600-foot-deep gorge, its bottom drowned in vegetation.

Dr. Coy was a veteran of the gorge as well. He'd spent countless weekends "boondocking," as he called it: hacking through rhododendron thickets, crawling into caves, edging up and down cliff faces. He goes in search of prehistoric petroglyphs and 150-year-old saltpeter mines. (Red River Gorge was an important source of saltpeter for gunpowder in the War of 1812.) On this steamy day in late May, Dr. Coy wanted to show me one of his favorite spots. After a short hike along the rim, the three of us headed downward, carefully stepping over thick tree roots and skidding down slopes greased with dead leaves. Suddenly the trees seemed to part and before us opened a natural amphitheater.

We had come to one of the gorge's spacious rock houses. A trickle of water fell from the overhang above, splattering us as we entered the cool shelter. Ceiling and walls were moist with water percolating down through layers of sandstone, slowly dissolving the rock. The floor of the rock house was covered with heaps of ash and dirt, debris left by pothunters. Woodland Indians had used the shelter some one to two thousand years ago. If any artifacts had been left behind, they were gone now after years of scavenging. But Dr. Coy beckoned me to a pile of stones which he began to dismantle. With a leafy branch, he swept off the flat rock at the bottom of the pile to reveal in the half-light an etched set of animal tracks. It was one of a limited number of rock carvings left behind by eastern Indians. Though not as dramatic or complex as the Indian petroglyphs of the Southwest, these crude designs were nonetheless just as powerful at the moment of discovery, haunting the woods with the spirits of past inhabitants. "This was a beautiful place to live," Dr. Coy reflected. "It had all the features of home—shelter, water, good exposure. Can't you imagine Indians living here?"

All across the South, the woods do resonate with past human activity—mining, lumbering, Civil War skirmishes, Indian and pioneer migrations, homesteading, and hunting. Rare is the hollow or ridgeline that lacks some fragment of history. Yet almost 300 miles south of Red River Gorge, where the Cumberland Plateau crosses the northwest corner of Georgia, lies a piece of country that largely has been left

Spray surges from clefts in limestone (pages 56-57), creating whistling sounds. Thus Florida's Blowing Rocks Beach earns its name, though the rocks whistle only when waters churn from storms. Owned and protected by the Nature Conservancy, the 1 1/4-mile stretch along the southern tip of Jupiter Island remains one of Florida's few wild beaches. Sea turtles come ashore on Jupiter to lay eggs on summer evenings. Wild limes, mangroves, and coco plums flourish in the salt spray and humidity.

untouched by human events. Just below the Tennessee-Georgia border on a ridgeline known as Lookout Mountain, the land suddenly falls away to reveal a gaping 2,000-foot chasm, one that is ribbed with great sandstone bluffs on its upper tier, suffused in forest at the bottom, and alive with the sight and sound of water falling over cliffs.

The first time I saw Cloudland Canyon, viewing it from high on its eastern rim, my gaze swooped across its impressive distances. Below me the cliff walls plunged hundreds of feet into a green web of trees, under which Daniel Creek and Bear Creek, sculptors of the gorge, flowed unseen. To the north the forested canyon walls became less precipitous, merging gradually into the hazy levelness of Lookout Valley. Cloudland Canyon takes its name from the days, usually in winter, when the mile-long gorge is swaddled in clouds. On a late spring morning, however, with an ocean of blue sky overhead, the canyon lay in full, riveting view.

Unlike the canyon walls of the Southwest, where colorful strata of rock are bared to sight, graphically depicting stages of the earth's geologic history, the rock walls of the more intimate eastern gorges are nearly always obscured by dense covers of vegetation. At Cloudland Canyon, however, the clear view of massive, protruding bluffs, too sheer to permit a takeover of trees, lends the gorge a kind of rugged grandeur not often encountered east of the Rockies.

The solitary ranger on duty at Cloudland Canyon State Park told me that few signs exist of people ever seriously inhabiting or working the gorge, though he guessed that at some time Cherokee Indians and early settlers must have hunted there. Today a few miles of hiking trail lead into the depths to two enchanting waterfalls. From all the evidence, Cloudland Canyon is a showcase of nature that has existed—and still exists—just to be looked at.

In the winter of 1811-12, naturalist John James Audubon was traveling on horseback across the Kentucky plains when suddenly "the ground rose and fell in successive furrows like the ruffled waters of a lake," as he would write in his journal. The earth "waved like a field of corn before the breeze." Audubon had experienced one of three shock waves that would shake the entire eastern third of the country between December 1811 and February 1812. Set off by tectonic disturbances in an ancient rift zone beneath the central Mississippi River Valley, the New Madrid Earthquake—lent its name by a Missouri town near the epicenter—unleashed awesome seismic waves. Geologists estimate they would have registered as high as 8.7 on the Richter scale—more powerful than the catastrophic San Francisco quake of 1906.

While church bells were set ringing in Boston and clocks stopped in Natchez, the scene near the epicenter was distinctly more violent. Sand geysers shot into the air; fissures opened in the earth; riverbanks collapsed; acres of forest toppled; and waterfalls and huge waves formed on the Mississippi. Across the river from New Madrid, the land beneath a cypress swamp sank. Water from the flooding Mississippi and dammed-up tributaries began to fill the subsided area. A lake was born.

In the quiet northwestern corner of Tennessee, Reelfoot Lake, 175 years later, still bears signs of its cataclysmic origins. From the irregular shoreline of the ten-mile-long body of water, I could see groves of bald cypress trees in the middle of the lake—Tennessee's only large stand of these stately trees so common to the South. Elsewhere I saw stark fields of jagged stumps—remnants of the 19th-century forest. Because of its bizarre appearance, the lake begged to be explored. So I hired a guide, John "Son" Cochran, a wiry Tennessean. In Son's johnboat we left one afternoon from the Samburg town dock on Reelfoot's southern shore and soon were slapping across the lake named after a legendary Chickasaw chief whose clubfoot caused him to reel when he walked.

Generations of duck hunters and fishermen have named every feature of the lake. With a hot May sun burning overhead, we furrowed through Nation's Ditch, a channel dredged across a willow-choked delta; maneuvered around the Palestine Stumps, an expanse of trees snapped in two by the earthquakes; and drifted into Buzzard Slough, where a patch of cypress offered shade. "Up here's where I've been catching fish," Son drawled. "I've been getting 100 bluegill a day." He watched me scribbling notes. "But, now, you usually don't tell nobody about your fishing beds. Sometimes not even your own family."

Continuing our circuit of Reelfoot, we chugged through flats of lily pads, skirted nearly submerged stumps that looked like alligator brows, and cruised down a ditch bisecting dank, dark woods. Great blue herons exploded from limbs as we passed, and largemouth bass lunged out of the water and fell back with a splash. Up to Brewer's Bar and down through Burnt Woods; past Horse Island and by Katie's Gourd; across Starve Pond and into Big Ronaldson Slough. After creeping through the murky slough, its water stained tobacco brown, the air as clammy as in a laundry, we reemerged into the open. Fresh air swept over our faces as if poured from a pitcher above. All in all, I'd never seen anything quite like Reelfoot Lake. It could adopt any number of guises: swamp, delta, river, glade, or bayou. There was none of the monotony of being out in the middle of a big, featureless sheet of water. As a friend of Son's remarked to me back on shore, "Reelfoot is nature packed up all in one big deal."

Rich in animal life, the Reelfoot area boasts some 240 species of birds. Each fall, thousands of waterfowl migrate here. The lake also provides a winter haven for some 200 bald eagles. And its woodlands and marshes are alive with mink, muskrats, foxes, and other furbearers. Come spring, Reelfoot Lake is invaded by anglers. The only large natural lake in Tennessee (the rest were made by dams), Reelfoot lures the angler with its century-old reputation as one of the South's most productive fish hatcheries. Home to more than 50 species, the lake is abundant with such sport fish as largemouth bass, catfish, bluegill, and crappie. I was astounded by the triple-figure catches reported by fishermen. "Don't you get bored catching that many fish?" I asked a Memphis businessman on holiday as he carried off a plastic garbage bag stuffed with the fillets of 150 bluegill. "Son," he replied, "do you get tired of breathing?"

Faced with such mania, I went fishing myself, having convinced old-timer Lexie Leonard, who runs boat tours for Reelfoot Lake State Park, to accompany me. I rented a "stump jumper," also known as a Reelfoot Lake boat, a canoe-size craft designed specially for the lake's peculiarities. The boat's flat, wide bottom and tilting rudder permit it to slide handily off the thousands of stumps and logs that lurk just beneath the surface in the shallow lake. (Depth ranges only four to eight feet.)

Revving the engine, I arrowed off toward Tri Timber, a spread of tall cypresses growing out of the water. Before 1811 these trees had probably stood on the bank of a sluggish stream. Lexie baited the hooks with crickets and, having nestled up to the ribbed skirt of a shady cypress, we hung the rods over the side and let the afternoon take us gently by the hand. The calm of an angler's day on Reelfoot contrasts sharply with the stormy episodes that characterize the lake's history. In 1899 a developer undertook an unsuccessful scheme to drain the lake and farm its bottom. Some years later a land company tried to make the lake private property and charge local fishermen royalties for taking out their catches. A gang of vigilantes murdered a company official before peace was struck.

Today the lake and much of its shoreline are public property, administered by the state park and a national wildlife refuge. But problems remain. The latest stems from the state of Tennessee's intent to lower the level of the lake to ease its grave siltation problem. Local fishermen, and residents involved in the tourist trade, many of whose families go back four or five generations on Reelfoot Lake, have gone to court to attempt to block the temporary drawdown. The locals almost unanimously fear that the state's plan would ruin their businesses and kill large numbers of fish and trees, all of which the state denies.

But such feuds and worries were wasted on Lexie and me as we inhabited that serene, timeless bubble that forms so easily around people fishing. With Lexie sculling the boat from the bow, we drifted through the watery cypress jungle, lazily catching a bluegill here, a crappie there, attributing the greatest wisdom to our underwater prey, holding out for the next tree, the next cricket, the next half hour. "Let 'im run," Lexie called once when a fish took my hook, his voice tinged with fondness and excitement.

An ornery-sounding chorus of frogs in a nearby patch of lily pads finally reminded us that evening was approaching. As we started back to shore, streaks of lightning tattooed a dark cloud above us, and rain began to fall. Lightning flashed again. Who knows, I mused, remembering Reelfoot's apocalyptic beginnings, maybe the rain would continue for days, even months, and Lexie and I then would float our stump jumper out over a brand-new world.

Cascading Cumberland Falls in eastern Kentucky projects a double rainbow. After the turmoil of the falls, the Cumberland River (below) flows placidly to the southeast. Declared a Kentucky Wild River for 16.1 miles, and thus protected by the state, the river wends its way past hemlock, hickory, laurel, and maple at the western edge of the Appalachians. Nearby, the Cumberland Gap, found by Thomas Walker in 1750, enabled pioneers to pass westward through the East's mountain barrier.

C atawba rhododendron blossoms crown star bursts of greenery. Rhododendron thickets up to ten feet high—"laurel hells"—frustrated Cumberland explorers. Native to North America, the shrub thrives in the Southeast's moist, mild climate and acidic, humus-rich soil.

65

Headlights glow as a car emerges from the darkness of Kentucky's Nada Tunnel. Originally used by logging trains, the tunnel now gives autos on Highway 77 passage through the 120-foot-high sandstone wall. Trees crowd in on the man-made tunnel and the neighboring Natural Bridge (opposite), which the Lexington and Eastern Railroad first billed as a tourist attraction in 1895. Natural Bridge, near the Red River Gorge, numbers among some 100 natural arches found within 30 square miles, second in total only to those of Utah's Colorado Plateau region.

Old ways linger in the hills of Kentucky, where Charlie Mills, 72, and his mule Ellen plow a one-acre vegetable garden on his farm near Mills Creek. PAGES 70-71: Seen from rocky Pinnacle Overlook—legendary site of Cherokee war councils—clouds pour through the Cumberland Gap.

THE MIDWEST

Scenic Surprises of the Heartland

Daunting Great Lakes, tallgrass prairies stretching to the horizon, tortuous badlands—this and more greeted explorers and settlers of America's heartland. "Boundless and beautiful," wrote poet William Cullen Bryant of the grasslands that once rolled from the Appalachians to the Rockies, from Texas into Canada. Fields of native grasses (opposite) dance in the ever present winds in the Flint Hills of Kansas, largest remaining tract of tallgrass in the Midwest. There, the prairie wild rose (above) unfolds under a summer sun. PAGES 74-75: Emptiness reigns on the Konza Prairie in the Flint Hills.

DAVID MUENCH

THE MIDWEST

By Bill Richards
Photographs by
    Philip Schermeister

America's heartland holds surprises that delight the eye and capture the imagination. Surf-battered cliffs and dense woodlands lend a timeless quality to shores of Lake Superior. Vestiges of a vast domain, the Loess Hills of Iowa and the Konza Prairie retain the untamed character of America's tallgrass region. In the Black Hills of South Dakota, long held sacred by Plains Indians, the beauty and the mystery of the mountains still inspire reverence in those who behold them.

From where I stood, high on the trail above Lake Superior's northwest coast, the stockade below at Grand Portage was no more than a child's flimsy stick fort stacked along the shore. Superior, the color of pearl and flat to the horizon, was completely empty and looked very cold. It wasn't hard to imagine a canoe filled with voyageurs stroking for shore after muscling their way across hundreds of miles of the lake the Indians called Gitche Gumee— the "shining Big Sea Water." To those bone-weary eastern traders, nearly three centuries ago, landfall and Grand Portage must have seemed like the promise of long life itself.

And riches. For toward this same destination from the opposite direction came far-ranging fur traders, staggering under a winter's take of beaver pelts gathered from streams and lakes all the way to the Rockies. Fashion-conscious Europe would be served—for a price.

It was here at Grand Portage that America's first major continental trading ground developed, where merchant-adventurers from the East swapped their finished goods for natural riches from the West. For more than a century, first the French, later the English, trudged up this narrow trail, on their way to the great trapping grounds of the upper Midwest and whatever else lay out there beyond. The names would fill an explorers' guide: Sieur de la Vérendrye, Alexander Henry, David Thompson, Alexander Mackenzie, many more.

Superior, their highway, is the largest freshwater lake on earth, the deepest, coldest, and most remote of the five Great Lakes. I had come to this shore on a trek across America's midlands. The trail would lead me through tallgrass prairies, along the bluffs of the winding Missouri River, and into South Dakota's mystical Black Hills. Now, as I stood literally in the footprint of Lake Superior's history, the north shore seemed to me to have maintained much of the wild and lonely visage that greeted the early voyageurs.

Some things, however, have changed. Driving along U.S. Highway 61, tracing the track along the lake's rocky shoreline from the Canadian border to Duluth, I passed streams of modern adventurers. But they carried their canoes. Strapped across the tops of an endless procession of cars and vans, the small upended boats reminded me of a parade of cockaded caps. Most were headed into the interior of Minnesota's northeastern "Arrowhead," toward the Boundary Waters Canoe Area and some of the nation's finest wilderness canoeing.

Along Superior's northern shores, timber wolves still leave footprints in winter. And moose regularly stroll out of the north woods' jack pine and aspen in any season. "Not many golf courses have a moose hazard on their fifth hole, but we do," boasted Walter Mianowski, mayor of Grand Marais. The 1,300 residents of the quiet Minnesota community were just emerging from a six-month winter when I visited. By summer, Grand Marais' population would rocket to more than 5,000.

Walter arrived on the north shore 32 years ago, out of Pennsylvania to join a construction crew and build docks for the big boats that carried

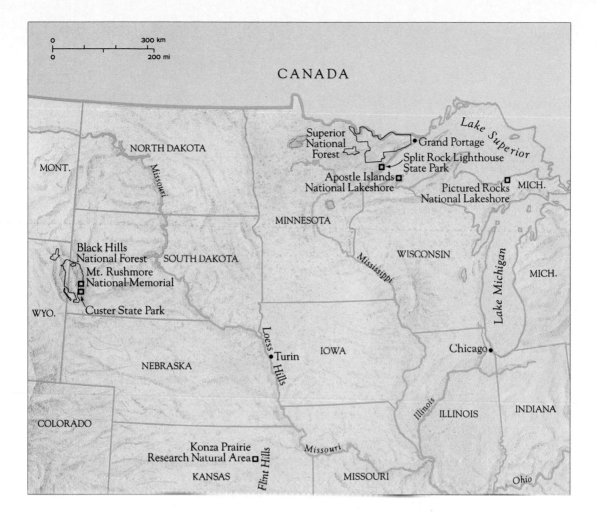

iron ore down the lake from Minnesota's Mesabi Range. When the work was done he stayed on. "I found peace and tranquillity and black flies and mosquitoes," he said with a contented chuckle. "How could I go back to Pittsburgh after that?"

Others found different allurements. As I drove along the lakefront I slowed to read the names on the mailboxes . . . Swenson . . . Andersen . . . Peterson. Records show that more than a fifth of the populations of Norway and Sweden emptied out during the final decades of the 19th century; a quarter of a million from Sweden alone chose to come to Minnesota. And many of them settled along Superior's north shore, where there was plenty of pine to be cut and iron to be mined. Near the little community of Lutsen, I passed a wedding party, heirs perhaps to those tough, early immigrants. A proud sign on the limousine bearing the newly married couple read, "Honk if you're Norwegian."

For the most part, Grand Portage and the north shore settlements have relinquished their original commercial role. But they were forerunners of the Midwest's destiny. Chicago, my home, along with the other great cities of the midland, are their stepchildren. Perhaps that is because the Midwest has no great mountain barriers, no impassable edges to hinder the commercial ebb and flow of a continent. Indeed, sometimes it seems nature itself was just passing through: Glaciers, volcanoes, and great seas have all come and gone from here, leaving just tantalizing clues to their presence. At times, only the wind seems to be permanent in the Midwest.

"Even in summer, when your warm air hits your cool water, the wind can blow up so fast you can get eight-foot waves in minutes. The fishermen say you'll see another day—if you survive the first half hour." I was getting a Lake Superior weather lesson from Bill Gordon as we sat outside his one-room log cabin on Manitou Island.

Manitou is one of the Apostle Islands. The islands are scattered across some 600 square miles of southwestern Lake Superior, like a handful of pebbles tossed by a giant hand. The 22 Apostles, save two, have been under the aegis of the National Park Service since they were designated a national lakeshore in 1970.

A barrel-chested man—part Chippewa, part French—Bill has been coming to Manitou for most of his 60 years. In the 1950s, he worked out of a bachelors' fishing camp that had been on the island since the late 1800s. When the Park Service came along, he joined up, and now he's comfortably ensconced back in the old camp.

Bill instructs a stream of visitors in the old-time ways of catching and smoking Superior's whitefish and lake trout. He is a natural teacher. Youngsters' eyes go wide when he describes the art of setting nets under four feet of ice in the middle of winter. (You drill two holes and slide the nets into place beneath the ice on a framework of timber.) "I guess after all these years I know the bottom the way you see the top," he says. Bill is still a pretty good fisherman and smokehouse operator. I ate some of his whitefish, brine-soaked and smoked over hard green maple, and right now, as I sit in Chicago, I find myself hungering for another bite.

One crisp sunny morning I packed a lunch and joined Jim Keller at the dock in Bayfield, Wisconsin, for a most unusual tour of the Apostles. Jim knows boats: He pilots them for a living, hauling tourists around the islands for the Park Service. But this 29-year-old sailor's true interest lies deep beneath Superior's cold waters.

"There are 21 major commercial shipwrecks scattered around the islands," he told me as we cast off. "Tugs, schooners, side-wheelers, right on up to the 373-foot ore carrier *Sevona*, which foundered off Sand Island in a September storm in 1905." In addition to his navigating skill, Jim is a scuba diver, a historian, and a writer. He wrote a book a couple of years ago—*The "Unholy" Apostles*—that gives the precise location and sad tale of each of these wrecks.

"If you look straight down right . . . there, that's the *Fedora*," Jim said, piloting our boat near the edge of Basswood Island. Sure enough, as I peered down into the clear water, the ghostly outlines of an ore ship emerged a dozen feet below. Superior's icewater has preserved the oak and iron skeleton of the 282-foot *Fedora* on the sandy bottom, much as she was when she settled in a shower of spark and flame on a chill September night 85 years ago.

Fedora's skipper, an experienced lake hand named Frank A. Fick, recounted the story after a cold night on the island. His ship, bound for a load of iron ore in Ashland, Wisconsin, caught fire steaming through the Apostles. In minutes the brisk lake wind fanned the flames from stem to stern. With no hope of rescue, Captain Fick aimed the *Fedora* full speed toward the mainland opposite Basswood. A frantic leap for the lifeboats saved all 17 of the crew and the two passengers.

A reporter for the *Ashland Daily Press* offered this graphic description of the *Fedora*'s remains the next day: "The fire consumed everything of wood above the water line, and her frame remains a twisted and contorted mass of ribbons and beams, a most gruesome sight indeed."

The *Fedora*'s grim underwater remains couldn't deaden the Apostles' exhilarating beauty. From our boat, Jim and I watched white-winged squadrons of sailboats, spinnakers taut, coasting between the islands. At the edge of Basswood Island Jim tied our boat fast to a birch tree, and we went looking for the island's past. During the last century, loggers stripped the Apostles and much of the rest of the north woods all but bare. Timber barons built handsome mansions on Bayfield's hillsides, and the islands' woods rang with the sound of axes chipping white pine. The Apostles grew out after the loggers moved on, but mostly with a canopy of maples, oak, and birch. These days, the hardwoods have all but replaced the original stands of solemn pine, transforming the islands into beacons of color each fall.

In a sun-dappled hollow near the south end of Basswood, we came upon what looked like the leftovers of a Maya temple. Huge stone blocks, some as much as eight feet long, lay scattered around the site. A deep pool of black water filled the bottom of a quarry where giant steps had been chiseled into the hillside. In a sense these *are* temple remains. But the quarrymen spoke mostly Gaelic or Swedish, and the ocher stone went to build civic and commercial temples in cities like Chicago, Minneapolis, and St. Paul. In the 1880s, some 600 men worked the nation's biggest brownstone quarry here. Their stone went into the old Milwaukee Court House and Chicago's stately Tribune Tower. It is said here with some pride that Basswood stone rebuilt Chicago after its great fire.

I confess I find it hard to imagine the Apostles as they were then. I can't picture the air filled with the snarl of sawmills or the mist of quarry dust. Bald eagles soar above these islands now, and black bear den up in the deep silence of winter. Bill Gordon, who has been a logger as well as a fisherman here, says he prefers the islands the way they are now. "There's a peace to them after all these years," he says.

Of course Superior, as many a woozy lake traveler can attest, is never really at peace. The greatest of the Great Lakes fights an endless battle against the confines of its shoreline. At Pictured Rocks National Lakeshore, on Michigan's rugged Upper Peninsula, Fred Young and I came upon some disturbing evidence of Superior's fury during a visit to the 114-year-old whitewashed brick lighthouse that marks Au Sable Point.

Fred is a lean, reserved National Park Service ranger, a New Jersey native who has spent the last 14 of his 46 years at Pictured Rocks. He laid out the trail that rambles for miles along the edge of Pictured Rocks' carved sandstone bluffs, and sometimes, on his days off, he still walks the beach here just to savor its beauty. But he was clearly awed by the gouged and torn shoreline around the 107-foot lighthouse. "We had a bad storm in November. Lasted a couple of days, but I had no idea . . .," Fred said, his words trailing off as he inspected the damage.

The lighthouse, which marks an especially dangerous sandstone shoal off the point, was manned until 1958 and now operates automatically. Fred said the Park Service plans to buttress the shore with concrete to preserve the historic light and its surrounding buildings from the encroaching lake. "We're racing the lake, and I'm not sure we're winning," he said dubiously when we left.

Not long after dawn the next day, I hiked Fred's trail. "Each time you come around another bend," he had promised, "you'll find something even better than what you left behind." In retrospect, I think Fred was understating. From the top of the Pictured Rocks' 200-foot cliffs I looked down onto broad arches and solitary pinnacles sculpted from the shore as far as I could see. Superior's breakers—translucent green in the morning light—boomed as they rolled into deep caves below. The rocks themselves were a mural of colors, streaked red, blue, and green by iron and copper; white and orange by limestone and lichen.

I met no other hiker on my four-mile walk. But at a small white-sand beach, blown onto the top of a bluff by the wind, I stopped to measure my observations against those of another traveler, a writer and artist named A. L. Rawson, who compiled a chatty account of his visit to Pictured Rocks in 1867 for *Harper's New Monthly Magazine*. Rawson pronounced the shore a "Fairyland of the Great Lake," and he concluded: "Not all the wonders of the Grotto of Antiparos, or the splendors of Fingal's Cave in Staffa, or the magnificence of the Rocks of Etretat in Brittany, can compare with the unrivaled and peculiar glories of the Pictured Rocks of Lake Superior."

For those early travelers who turned south rather than risk the Great Lakes' perils, another inland sea waited. Oceans of grass, some taller than a man, taller than a horse—taller in spots than a man *and* his horse—stretched from the Appalachian forests to the foothills of the Rockies. Some marveled: "*Belles préries,*" sang Père Louis Hennepin after he traversed the valley of the Illinois River in 1683. Others didn't: "A desert—a barrier . . . placed by Providence to keep the American people from a thin diffusion and ruin," said Zebulon Pike, emerging in 1805 from the grasslands of what would become Nebraska and Kansas. I tend to side with Hennepin, though there *(Continued on page 88)*

(Continued on page 88)

Sculptured by time and weather, Cathedral Spires soar above stands of spruce and ponderosa pine in the Black Hills of South Dakota. Lofty peaks and sky-piercing pinnacles are common in these mountains, which rise abruptly from the gently rolling midwestern plains. Gen. George A. Custer, who explored the Black Hills in 1874, reported on the "enchanting scenery." Today, hiking trails and scenic highways give access to the magic of this landscape.

DAVID MUENCH

Monumental work of art, the presidential portraits of Mount Rushmore gaze steadfastly upon the Black Hills. Sculptor Gutzon Borglum and his crews dynamited away some 450,000 tons of granite to carve the faces of Washington, Jefferson, Theodore Roosevelt, and Lincoln. Each face measures approximately 60 feet from forehead to chin. Said Borglum, "A monument's dimensions should be determined by the importance . . . of the events commemorated."

A spens wear the vivid green of new growth in Black Hills National Forest. More than a million acres, the forest abounds in deer, elk, pronghorn, mountain goats, and big horn sheep. Forests blanket the Black Hills, the darkish cast of evergreens giving the region its name.

is precious little belle prérie left in Illinois. But in the Flint Hills of central Kansas an oasis of tallgrass prairie remains. More than 8,600 acres of the Konza Prairie wave in the wind at the truckers and travelers rumbling past on Interstate 70. As their name implies, the Flint Hills are a hard and inhospitable place. Their rocky soil discouraged farmers, but provided plenty of material for arrowheads for visiting Indians. "I expect this is what the first settlers saw when they got here," said Lloyd Hulbert, as we walked through grasses that brushed our shoulders. Prairie ecologist Hulbert and a group of fellow Kansas State University scientists, together with the Nature Conservancy, were responsible for purchasing and stitching together the swatches of prairie that make up the Konza. I visited with Lloyd shortly before his death early in 1986.

"I've always been fascinated with any wild land, and a lot more people are becoming interested too these days," Lloyd said. But he added this caution: "The prairie isn't like the redwoods, which simply awe you with their size. You've got to learn something about a prairie to really understand and enjoy it."

Here are a few things that Lloyd and others taught me about the prairie: Just half a square meter of prairie sod may hold nearly 13 miles of packed root structure (which may explain why a lot of early sodbusters busted their plows when they tackled the tallgrass). In wet years following a dry spell, big bluestem, the king of the prairie tallgrass, can reach more than eight feet in height, creating a grass wall that sometimes left Kansas cattlemen standing on their saddles looking for their Herefords. And prairie fire, while seemingly fierce, doesn't harm the roots of grasses, in fact leaves them stronger by eliminating competitors, like trees.

"The prairie is so efficient in its use of nutrients that it is the ultimate standard by which to compare our present-day manipulated agricultural systems," said Tim Seastedt, a Kansas State prairie ecologist. Tim believes that someday plant geneticists may end up tapping the prairie for the genes that will produce the supercrops of the future.

I understood more of the tallgrass prairie's unique blend of toughness and fragility during a visit to the Konza before sunup one warm spring morning. As I hiked through the grass, alone under a full moon, I watched the wind rippling across the hills of open prairie. Willa Cather provided my favorite description of such a scene when she wrote: "The whole country seemed . . . to be running."

In a small hilltop blind in the midst of this vast whispering sea, I settled down to wait. Suddenly I heard a soft sort of yodeling sound. Singly at first, then in dozens, partridge-size birds fluttered out of the grass and began to strut, hop, and dance on the open ground while making a drumming noise. These greater prairie chickens, an endangered species but still prolific on the Konza, perform this mating ritual for several weeks each spring. I watched the dance, riveted to my ringside seat through the sunrise. Then, as magically as they had appeared, the birds filtered back into the grass and disappeared. On my way off the prairie that morning I searched hard, but couldn't find a single bird.

"Sure they're there," Flint Hills cowboy Dusty Anderson assured me later, when I wondered aloud at what I saw, or thought I saw. Sixty-three, lean and long as a stalk of big bluestem, Dusty herds cows sent from as far away as Texas to fatten up on the prairie's rich grass. "I've kicked up prairie chickens dozens of times riding through the tallgrass," he said. "They sure do look pretty when they do that dance, don't they?"

Like the Flint Hills of Kansas, Iowa's Loess Hills are another obstinate streak of hilly landscape stretched across the flat Midwest. The Loess (pronounced luss) Hills meander along the east side of the Missouri River all the way from Sioux City, where the river zigs south, to Kansas City, where it zags back to its original eastward heading. In fact, some say that if the Missouri didn't wander so much the hills probably wouldn't be there at all.

During the last ice age, between 24,000 and 14,000 years ago, when the Missouri was a gruel of glacial silt, the hills were only low tree-studded rises left over from a far earlier glacial era. In winter, when the glaciers slowed their melting and the river dropped, the silt in the runoff settled along the broad bottomland, only to be lofted into the air by the prevailing west-to-east winds. The flying silt blew smack against the rises, piled higher and higher until, voilà, hills in Iowa.

"Like a snow fence in winter," is the way geologist Art Bettis describes it. Art works for the Iowa Geological Survey and is an expert on the Loess Hills. Windblown silt can be found piled an extraordinary 150 feet deep in places here, he said. Only in China, primarily along the Yellow River, can similar deposits be found. Because it travels on the wind, loess is generally uniform in size—bigger than clay particles, smaller than sand. "It's great stuff to farm," Art said, "except the hills are so steep in most places you'd need a ladder."

But the farmers' loess is the prairie fancier's gain. Early one May morning in Sioux City I climbed into Dr. William Blankenship's Chevy pickup, and we headed into the surrounding Loess Hills for a wildflower tour. Besides practicing medicine, Bill has written on prairie wildflowers for the *Sioux City Journal,* and he happily admits to being a "prairie nut." One day in 1979, while a real estate agent was showing him a building lot in Sioux City, Bill spotted a patch of open prairie on a nearby hillside, covered with trash and motorcycle ruts. He didn't buy the lot, but he helped raise $80,000 toward buying and reviving the prairie. "It's one of two urban prairies I know of in the United States," he told me proudly.

Around Sioux City the hills wore the first soft green velvet of spring prairie, and cloud shadows raced up and down the steep slopes. Bill headed triumphantly for a patch of pasqueflowers hugging the ground. Pasqueflowers go by a confusing number of aliases— wild crocus, lion's beard, prairie smoke. No matter what the name, it is a jewel of a flower, a spray of pale lavender blossoms that resemble shy tulips huddled against the soil. "Spring doesn't officially arrive around here until the pasqueflowers begin blooming," Bill said.

Harsh sunlight and constant wind tend to desiccate the hills, leaving them almost desert-like in spots and causing botanical oddities to show up. Bill pointed out purple locoweed and yucca plants, both dryland natives usually found much farther west. But he was disappointed that we couldn't locate a three-inch-tall, olive-green fern, a new species that he and several fellow botanists discovered here in 1981. Some Iowa biologists call it the "hills fern," in honor of the Loess Hills.

"You expect to find ferns in wet, shady places, so we were really surprised to find this one here," Bill said. "Just knowing something that rare is out there makes these hills extra special."

When dry, loess bonds tightly to itself. Highway engineers take advantage of this when they cut roads through the hills, leaving the sides of the cuts almost vertical so they stay dry and in place. But when it gets wet, loess can't even hold its own weight. During heavy rainstorms the soil seems to melt away. Such erosion helps sculpt the hills along the Missouri, leaving a scalloped pattern of dramatic bluffs and saddles.

Driving south through the hills, I pulled over to read a weathered roadside sign in the little community of Turin, Iowa. "Turin Man Archaeological Discovery 1955," it said. The sign offered no details, and no one was around to explain, so I called Duane Anderson, Iowa's state archaeologist, and asked about the sign. Duane chuckled and filled me in on the story of "George," the Turin Man.

Quarry operators working in the loess of Turin's gravel pit in 1955 uncovered remains of a human skeleton. The county coroner at first thought the skeleton was that of a local man named George, who had been missing since 1940. But archaeologists who were called in declared that "George" was possibly 9,000 years old, making him the oldest human skeleton ever discovered in North America.

Suddenly, little Turin was famous. "Anthropologists, archaeologists, *Life* magazine, everybody who was anybody showed up," Duane said. It took archaeologists 30 years to shake out the truth. "We used radiocarbon dating on the skeleton and it turned out to be the remains of an Indian about 5,000 years old." In 1985 Duane and other archaeologists reported on the skeleton's true identity. "The Turin Man was still a respectable scientific find," Duane says. "Even though he wasn't the oldest man any more, Turin's still proud of him."

Of all the conversation pieces the Loess Hills have provided Iowans, few rank with Russ Lindeman's Mount Crescent Ski Area. "When people see our sign they stop and tell us 'Gosh, you can't ski in Iowa,'" Russ said when I, too, stopped to gawk. His chalet-style house at the edge of the area's 2,000-foot run makes this part of the Loess Hills, just north of Council Bluffs, look more like Innsbruck than Iowa.

Russ proudly describes his ski slope as "the prettiest place in Iowa." I won't argue with that. When I looked out his kitchen window, as we visited over a cup of coffee, I could see a carpet of deep purple wildflowers waving in the breeze across the hillside. And each winter, when the wind turns cold and Russ cranks up his snow-making machines, some 20,000 Iowans and Nebraskans get a chance to schuss down the loess on what may be the world's only ski run built on a prairie.

Far to the west of Iowa, in South Dakota, I stood several days later on Harney Peak, the 7,242-foot summit of the mountains the Lakota Sioux Indians called *Paha Sapa*—Hills that are Black. Below me, red-tailed hawks chased each other in lazy circles across a frieze of splintered granite spires and bare-knuckled knobs and ridges. Dark ranks of ponderosa pine crept up out of shadowy canyons. I understood immediately why the Sioux and other Plains Indians believe these mountains to be holy and why one awed early visitor, a military officer, called them "the embodiment of the fullest idea of the mysterious and the unknown."

Nowadays, of course, tourists in the millions make their way into the Black Hills to view the presidential profiles sculptured on Mount Rushmore, or to park the station wagon for an hour or so at one or another of the roadside attractions, from snake farms to water slides. I have no special gripe with these oddities, but I suspect that most of these visitors miss the hills' true beauty.

Climbing Harney Peak, I chose the route that Gen. George A. Custer followed during his expedition here in 1874. "Every step of our march that day was amid flowers of the most exquisite colors and perfume," Custer wrote of the outing. The hardened campaigner was charmed by the hills. Glancing back during his trip up the peak, he reported a strange sight: "The men with beautiful bouquets in their hands, while the headgear of the horses was decorated with wreaths of flowers fit to crown a queen of May."

To be sure, Custer came to explore and conquer the Black Hills, not to praise them. Ten companies of the Seventh Cavalry, two of infantry, a squad of Indian scouts, and a military band—more than 1,000 troops in all—marched the length of the hills and back. When they emerged, Custer's report of gold discoveries touched off a prospectors' stampede. The solitude of the Paha Sapa was broken forever.

Most of the early Black Hills mining camps are long gone. But in Lead (pronounced leed), South Dakota, the famed Homestake Mine, biggest of them all, is still active. Some 35 million troy ounces of gold have come from the mine's spiderweb of tunnels deep beneath the Black Hills—worth nearly 15 billion dollars at today's prices. The Homestake Mining Company has owned and operated the mine since 1877, the year after it was discovered by prospectors Fred and Moses Manuel and their partner, Henry Harney. The three men sold their find to San Franciscan George Hearst and two others in what certainly ranks as one of the world's all-time bargains. The purchase price: $70,000.

How much gold remains in the Homestake? "Not everyone agrees with me, but I think there's at least as much left under these hills as has come out," speculates retired mining engineer Joel Waterland. Joel, who spent 40 years working for Homestake, told me the mine's gold veins stretch beyond the explored lode. "Nobody's found where they end," he said. Yet not everyone who came here looking for gold was lucky. Ezra Kind was one of the unfortunate ones. Near the town of Spearfish, in the northern Black Hills, I read Kind's last frantic message, scratched on a slab of sandstone at the base of Lookout Mountain in 1834: "Got all the gold we could carry, our ponys all got by the Indians. I hav lost my gun and nothing to eat and Indians hunting me."

Only a small granite tablet marks where Kind's message was found—53 years too late. Historians still debate whether it is authentic: How many of us would scratch a note to posterity with death lurking at the edge of the tree line? But real or concocted, Kind's message has one authentic note. It conveys the loneliness and desperation of a doomed man, with no help or hope in sight, only those dark piny ridges.

Outside Sturgis I pulled my car over for a long-distance look at Bear Butte, the sacred mountain of the Plains Indians. To geologists, the butte is a volcanic bubble, a 50-million-year-old lava blister. To the early white explorers crossing westward, the mountain was an unmistakable landmark, jutting 1,200 feet out of the plains at the northeastern edge of the Black Hills. But to the Indians it is simply the holy mountain. Here Sweet Medicine received the four sacred arrows representing the code of ethics that governs the Cheyenne. Here, too, legend holds, White Buffalo Calf Woman gave the Sioux their sacred calf pipe. The Mandan believe the mountain was the refuge that preserved the tribe during a great flood back in the mists of unwritten history. For untold centuries, the Kiowa, Arikara, Crow, Mandan, Sioux, Cheyenne, and other Indians of the plains knew this striking landform as a site of worship.

Martin High Bear calls Bear Butte "a powerful place," where visions occur and the spirits sometimes speak. The 66-year-old Sioux medicine man, who lives on the Cheyenne River Reservation, had just finished his annual pilgrimage to the mountain when we talked. He was disappointed that poor health had kept him from climbing to the top this year. "Instead, I prayed in the sweat lodge," he said. "Then I sent my spirits up with others to listen and to pray."

A path, built by the state of South Dakota over Indian protest, winds to the summit of Bear Butte. On it I passed the skeletons of several sweat lodges, small rounded huts made from lashed-up tree branches. A rising wind set hundreds of black, red, yellow, and white ribbons fluttering in the trees—"gifts to the spirits" from Indian pilgrims, Martin said.

No spirits spoke to me at the mountain's top. But it was indeed a powerful place. The lowest clouds seemed just out of reach, and a lone golden eagle hung in the hissing wind beyond the butte's edge. The Black Hills stretched to the horizon, as dark and impenetrable now as they have been for as long as man has come to this mysterious place. Perhaps the spirits were there on Bear Butte after all. All I needed to learn was how to listen.

In a luminous watercolor, neighboring islands Lucille, foreground, and Susie fringe a pastel Lake Superior. Uninhabited and accessible only by boat, the islands lie within a rocky archipelago edging the border between the United States and Canada. "It wasn't hard to imagine a canoe filled with voyageurs stroking for shore . . .," writes the author about Superior's wild northern coast. Largely untouched by man, this region looks much as it did centuries ago.

P rovince of wind and water, Lake Superior reveals its many-sided personality in restive surf and peaceful skies. Among the far-flung Apostle isles, waves lash the shore of Devils Island (below) in northern Wisconsin. Like puppets hanging on a string, herring gulls (opposite) glide on gentle winds.

*S*plit Rock Lighthouse
tops a 130-foot-high
basalt headland
overlooking western Lake
Superior. During the early
20th century the transport
of iron ore kept shipping
lanes busy. The flashing
light of Split Rock helped
ships navigate through the
treacherous waters and
unpredictable weather of
Superior, which has
claimed dozens of vessels.
Today the lighthouse, a
state historic site, no longer
shines a guiding beacon,
but informs visitors of the
lore of Lake Superior.

M ultihued language of autumn proclaims the season along Superior's shores, where the hardwood forests of northern Minnesota (below) raise a chorus of glorious voices. Evergreen and deciduous woodlands cover the northern lake region. The bright leaves of a serviceberry tree accent the Temperance River (opposite) as it tumbles through a gorge in Superior National Forest. Nearly three million canoeists, fishermen, backpackers, and other lovers of nature visit the national forest each year.

Spiky blossoms of wild lupine add a vivid hue to the woodland palette of Superior National Forest. In America's heartland, the fine details and broad strokes of nature's artistry—from a closeup view of delicate wildflowers to the panorama of the windswept badlands—can be found in the lakes, in the mountains, and in the prairies.

THE ROCKIES
Wild Realms of Solitude and Freedom

Pathfinders surmounted it; pioneers struggled across it; mountain men trapped, miners dug, and loggers chopped—yet the raw wonder of the continental barrier remains. Scarlet gilia (above) flares amid the Bitterroots in Idaho, showing why many call it skyrocket, firecracker, or trumpet. Rocky Mountain streams, descending, slice through Canyonlands National Park in Utah (opposite), where a photographer scans the geologic record exposed in layered sandstone. The bizarre shapes, which include Angel Arch and the Molar (pages 104-105), all yield to the rasp of wind and water, the stress of heat and frost.

THE ROCKIES

By Mark Miller
Photographs by David Hiser

*Peaks of granite crowning
spires of evergreen,
showers of steam in the
frozen hush of winter,
restless sands milled by the
winds, canyons haunted by
"ten thousand strangely
carved forms." From the
classic backcountry of
the Selway-Bitterroot
to the 200 active geysers
of Yellowstone, from
the high desert of Great
Sand Dunes National
Monument to steep-
walled Canyonlands, the
mountain states preserve
enclaves of contrast in
a tapestry of grandeur.*

It was the last day of a glorious Indian summer, warm and dry, the transpiration of trees filling the mile-high Idaho forest with a natural blue haze. The frame of my heavily loaded pack squeaked in rhythm with my gait as I hiked the Big Sand Lake Trail through stands of lodgepole pine, subalpine fir, and Engelmann spruce. Afternoon sunlight slanted through the trees in thick golden shafts. A raven's distant cry only heightened the sense of stillness. I was just four miles into the Selway-Bitterroot Wilderness of Idaho and Montana, yet, in truth, I was as far away from civilization as you can get in the northern Rockies.

Farther up the trail, my companion Jim Dolan, a forester working out of the Forest Service's regional office in Missoula, Montana, marched through the heat. I stopped to soak a handkerchief in the quietly trickling water of Big Sand Creek. Pressing the handkerchief to my face, I found the coolness a refreshing relief from the pine-scented heat. Easing out of the straps of my pack, I sat back against a tree and savored the peacefulness of this place. All around was pristine forest, virtually unmarked by man. The sense of seeing the living, ageless past, indeed of escaping time as we measure it, was thrilling.

This wilderness probably looked little different in 1805, when the first white men known to have seen it blazed a trail a few miles north of where I rested. Headed west through Idaho's Nez Perce Indian country, Meriwether Lewis and William Clark and their band of explorers called this terrain the most difficult encountered in their 18-month journey to the Pacific, complaining of "high mountains," "falling timber," and "ruged Knobs" that made progress "slow and extreemly laborious." Lewis noted a local plant whose bitter root the Flathead Indians considered a delicacy; from this plant the Bitterroot Range takes its modern name.

Though the Rocky Mountains run from British Columbia to New Mexico—a 1,900-mile-long geologic orchestration that includes some 50 mountain systems—my desire to see the Rockies as they were before the days of logging and road building led me to this rugged wilderness preserve. A straight line drawn some 400 miles south-southeast from Idaho's upper left corner to the city of Idaho Falls roughly traces the spine of the Bitterroot Range. Near its middle lies the Selway-Bitterroot, a 1.3-million-acre tract that reaches into Montana. What struck me most about the wilderness on first viewing was its deep, U-shaped valleys, gouged out by Pleistocene glaciers. Once virtually impassable for all but the most determined, it is now etched by more than 2,000 miles of primitive trails. On these, I spent three weeks probing its timeless interior.

As I rested by the creek, I checked my topographic map, retracing the four miles back to the Elk Summit Guard Station near Hoodoo Lake, our staging area of the previous day. Now, as I shouldered my pack and prepared to move on, it seemed odd that, though we had been on the trail only a few hours, yesterday seemed long ago. "You can lose your sense of time up here," Jim observed when I caught up with him. "No clocks, no traffic, no noises, no routines to mark the day. Only the angle

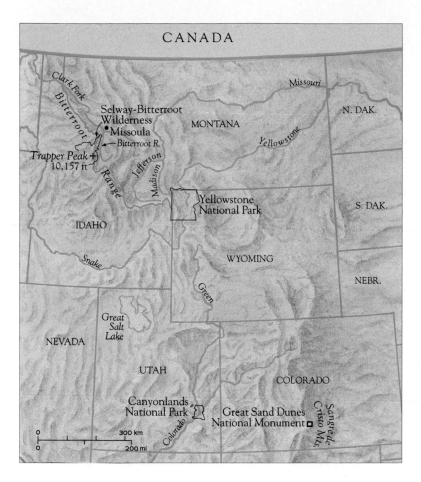

of the sun. I like it." We reached a trail junction that had no marker indicating the route to Blodgett Pass, the midpoint destination of our 26-mile hike. "You've got to be able to read a map in this country," Jim cautioned. "When you study a map and guide yourself, it makes your trip a lot more satisfying and memorable. Self-discovery is an important part of the wilderness experience."

The shadows were long when we reached our first night's campsite at Big Sand Lake. A bit footsore after only eight miles, I had to admire the hiking prowess of the legendary Bob Marshall, first recreation chief of the Forest Service and a founder of the Wilderness Society. Marshall once covered 29 snowy miles here in a single December day. He called it a "long walk." It was Marshall's preservationist campaign in the 1920s and '30s that helped spare parts of the Bitterroot, Clearwater, Lolo, and Nez Perce National Forests from logging and road building. This region remained an island in time until 1964, when Congress, noting its untrammeled character, included it in the nation's system of wild lands.

The evening at Big Sand Lake was peaceful, the stillness broken by an occasional snap from our fire and the squawking of "camp robbers"—hungry gray and Steller's jays. As the light dimmed, the forest colors merged to shades of dusky purple. Heat lightning flickered in the west.

The timbered ridges surrounding us made serrated silhouettes against the glowing sky. Reading by flashlight later, I could hear the faint patter of pine needles falling onto the fabric of my tent. Next morning, we woke to the steady snare-drumming of rain. Donning warm clothes and ponchos over thermal underwear, we ate breakfast beneath a tarpaulin. Our breath made steam. Cradling a cup of hot chocolate, Jim peered up at the unexpected clouds obscuring the peaks above us. "Weather forecasting in the Rockies," he said, "is a high-risk profession."

Scattering our fire's ashes and covering the spot with pine needles, we policed the campsite to erase all traces of our stopover. When we left Big Sand Lake we found a water-filled trough where the trail had been. For three hours we sloshed along, climbing 1,800 feet through stands of western larch and lodgepole pine. Gusts shook the thickly needled branches above us, bringing down additional showers. At 6,900 feet, the temperature stood below 40°F, and the season's first snowfall was powdering the peaks 2,000 feet above. The timber and understory were sparse, exposing the region's predominant gray granitic rock.

The last 300 feet up the switchback trail to Blodgett Pass reared steep as a barn roof. The footing was crumbly, forcing us to be constantly alert. Glances at the magnificent subalpine forest came at the risk of a nasty fall. Suddenly the trail leveled. We had reached the pass. Looking around, I was rewarded by a spectacular view of Blodgett Canyon, one of the region's most dramatic, its sheer, glacier-polished walls curving like a mammoth stone tub. Rainwater fell in feathery plumes from a dozen places along the canyon rim. The barren, snow-whitened pyramid of 8,648-foot Blodgett Peak rumbled softly with an echo of distant thunder.

That night, my last on the Blodgett Canyon Trail, I began to understand how this country subtly captivates. We had pitched our tents on the canyon floor in a grove of western red cedar. The rain had let up. After supper I knelt by a quiet pool where a feeding cutthroat trout sent silvery rings expanding across the water. Abruptly there came a sound like that of a waterfall, but it was only a rush of wind through thousands of evergreen boughs. In a nearby clearing, a mule deer grazed with two spotted fawns. From overhead came a soft grating as two ponderosas rubbed together. Pine needles spiraled down into the creek and were carried away. Just as suddenly, the wind died, and it was quiet again. I reflected that we would leave the trail tomorrow, emerging near the logging town of Hamilton. Already I missed the wilderness.

Three days later under sunny skies, I drove southwest from Conner, along the West Fork of the Bitterroot River, to the West Fork Ranger Station. There I met Bob Oset, a wilderness ranger who was covered with the grime of a day spent repairing a backcountry trail. Seated on the dented tailgate of a pickup, he scraped mud from his boots and tried to explain his unabashed love of wilderness. "I don't think you can convey the effect this country can have to someone who hasn't been here," he said. "Ultimately, you've got to experience it firsthand."

At West Fork, as at most major trailheads and ranger stations, a resource specialist was on duty to offer maps, guidebooks, garbage sacks, and advice on trail conditions. "Education on wilderness use before going into the backcountry is the best method of management," Bob insisted. "Once people are inside, we assume they'd rather not see us unless they need help. Solitude and freedom—that's the essence of a wilderness experience."

My last day in the Bitterroot country dawned pearly, as though the Northwest lay beneath an enormous abalone shell. The radio warned of an approaching snowstorm. I decided to take one last panoramic look at the Selway-Bitterroot before winter arrived in earnest.

Heading southwest from Conner, retracing my route along the Bitterroot River's West Fork, I left my car and started up the trail to Trapper Peak, at 10,157 feet the highest in the Selway-Bitterroot. The air was damp and carried the scent of wet stone. The trail's steady incline followed the wilderness boundary and skirted the eastern ridge of Boulder Valley. Reaching the summit several hours later, I stretched out on a lichen-flecked slab of granite. The sun came out for the first time, warm on my face. I looked west across a meringue of granite peaks and dark forest. Three weeks here had cleared my mind of clutter, the distractions of everyday life. The view, as Bob Marshall used to say, was "swell." I felt that I could stay forever. I was fit to return home.

T he snowstorm approaching the Bitterroots that day heralded one of the earliest blizzards there in recent history, bringing much of western Montana to a virtual halt. Despite its rigors, many people I met in that country urged me to return for a taste of a Rocky Mountain winter. The following January, I did, to one of America's most extraordinary winter locales, Yellowstone National Park, in Wyoming's northwestern corner.

Signed into existence in 1872 by President Ulysses S. Grant, roughly 60 miles square, Yellowstone is our oldest national park and wildlife sanctuary, and the site of the world's largest and most varied collection of hydrothermal phenomena. Most of its two million acres lie on a plateau timbered by lodgepole pine and ringed by 11,000-foot mountains. The park overlaps state lines to claim strips of Idaho and Montana.

The temperature was ten above at noon when I reached Yellowstone's north entrance at Gardiner, Montana, under a vivid blue sky. Sunlight glared from the snow covering the juniper- and aspen-studded hills, the trees looking like great pyramids of shaving cream. Yellowstone's information radio station predicted an overnight low of minus 25 as a ranger collected my entrance fee. "That's not bad," he grinned, hearing the news. "Back in 1933 it got down to minus 40. That's nippy." He waved me through the gate, and I drove on. Traffic was light, a single van ahead, two cars behind—a far cry from Yellowstone's legendary summer crowds. "Over two million visitors every year," said Greg Kroll, a public affairs officer at the Park Service's Yellowstone headquarters at

Mammoth Hot Springs. "In the past ten years, the most people we've had in winter is 108,000. Counted 85,000 last year."

From mid-December until mid-March, Yellowstone draws cross-country skiers, snowmobilers, snowshoers, and, believe it or not, campers. "Put down a tent with a wooden floor, light up a little propane heater, you're toasty," outfitter Dale Fowler assured me. "We have a saying up here: 'Pray for 40 below; it keeps out the riffraff.'" An Arkansas native, Dale has a brother who is a Yellowstone ranger. "He convinced me to come out here and take a look. I'd heard about the winters, and I was scared of 'em. That was in 1975. I'm still here."

In any season, Yellowstone's main attraction is its hydrothermal activity—"that place the old Methodist preacher used to threaten me with" to 19th-century trapper Joe Meek, who blundered into his first geyser basin while fleeing hostile Blackfeet. In winter, frigid temperatures make the hydrothermal phenomena particularly evident. Then the park's four main geyser basins vent dense clouds of steam from hissing fumaroles, burbling mud pots, and placidly overflowing pools—all humbler relatives of Yellowstone's 200 active geysers. When explorer John Colter brought back the first accounts of this incredible region in 1808, he was initially suspected of having lost his mind.

I checked into the Mammoth Hot Springs Hotel, one of two hotels in the park open in winter, then followed a boardwalk through a delicate snowfall to the steaming travertine terraces of the springs for which the hotel is named. A step-like fountain of overlapping formations covering an entire mountainside—built up over the centuries from deposits left by the mineral-rich water—the hot spring is evidence of the subterranean fires left over from the Rocky Mountains' creation.

The secret of the Shoshone Indians' "burning mountains" lies in Yellowstone's location atop an unusually thin spot in the earth's crust, possibly just four miles thick and cracked by the upward pressure of an underlying massive blister of molten rock perhaps 200 miles deep. This magma chamber is capped by fractured rock that superheats the endless supply of water percolating downward. The superheated water is forced back up through the rock fissures, gurgling to the surface as hot springs or blasting from the earth as geysers.

In Colter's day there were few winter trails through the Yellowstone, and he and his fellow trappers ran the risk of wandering off snowblind into oblivion. I chose my cross-country ski routes from more than a hundred miles of trail, including a 45-mile network groomed by the park. One day, skiing from Canyon Junction in the park's center, I chanced on an elk about 200 feet away. It was caught in a shoulder-deep snowdrift, nose emitting rapid bursts of steam, ribs showing, a wary eye on me. For most of Yellowstone's grazing animals, winter months are an exhausting, sometimes deadly ordeal. When the first heavy snow falls, elk, moose, and deer abandon the high country and join bison herds to forage in thermally heated areas and river valleys, existing in a precarious state of near starvation. Aware *(Continued on page 120)*

Framed by a rocky portal, the lazy Colorado freights its load of silt around Gooseneck Bend in the canyonlands region. Amid such fantasies in stone the explorer John Wesley Powell climbed up from the river "as men would from a well" to discover "ledges from which the gods might quarry mountains . . . cliffs where the soaring eagle is lost to view ere he reaches the summit."

PAGES 112-113: Snow-veined El Capitan takes a last look at itself as storm clouds gather at Little Rock Creek Lake in the sprawling Selway-Bitterroot Wilderness. Lying in a glacial cirque at the end of a rocky, brush-choked trail, the tarn lures but a few hundred visitors a year. Some high lakes may not know a human footfall in a decade.

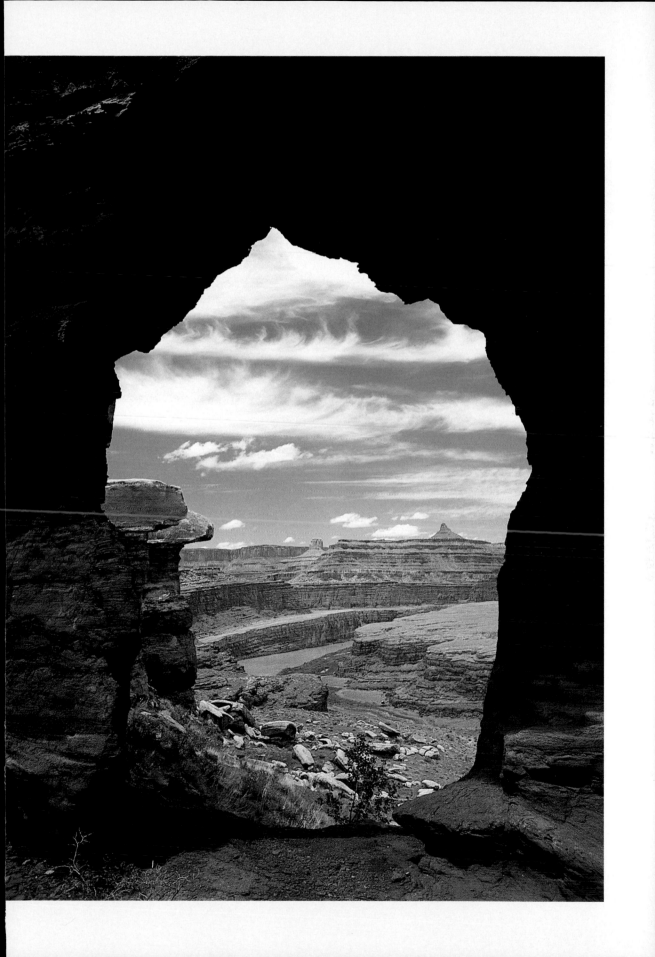

Rushing by scraggly slopes, the wild waters of the Selway River offer one of the most pristine floats in the lower 48, says federal forester Jim Dolan. Only one party of floaters may put in each day, and, according to Dolan, "They better know what they're doin'." With rock gardens and standing waves, the run at times ranges up to Class V, next to the most hazardous category of navigable rapids. Goat Creek Rapids, above, exemplifies a bit of the challenge, while the bunchberry at right displays a bit of the woodland beauty. PAGES 116-117: A hardy timberline dweller, the alpine larch leans out from its rocky perch to find a place in the sun.

utumn nips the high country in August, tinting a brush field of the Selway-Bitterroot. With the Crags behind him, a backpacker toils up from a headwaters cirque in the North Three Links drainage. No trail points the way. In this remote western corner, a wilderness hiker picks his own path.

that if I panicked the elk, it might needlessly expend energy essential to survival, I stayed motionless until it was able to reach the cover of the nearby forest. The trail from Canyon Junction took me past the rustic home of park winterkeeper Steve Fuller. An erudite and thoughtful man with a passion for books, and for life in the Yellowstone, he lives with his wife, Angela, and their two daughters in a century-old house. During the winter season, one of Steve's responsibilities is the exhausting job of clearing summer cabin roofs of snow that would otherwise collapse them. While he labors outdoors, British-born Angela manages the hotel at Mammoth. This year would mark their 14th in the park.

"It's a long time, but I feel as though I've just scratched the surface here," Steve told me one evening. "As you live in a landscape, you begin to associate places with past events, and these places acquire great power over you—like the animism of the Indian, which I have come to understand." Would he and Angela ever live anywhere else? "We've talked about it," he said, "but the attachment of self to land is profound, almost like an imprinting. At times the thought of separation seems almost like an amputation."

Could be, depending on where you end up," said Ranger Robert Schultz when I related Steve Fuller's sentiments about relocation. Formerly employed at the Old Faithful visitor center, Bob is now in charge of the visitor center in Colorado's Great Sand Dunes National Monument, the next stop on my exploration of the Rockies. "Terrain can differ greatly, yet you soon find yourself deriving the same satisfactions and pleasure you might have previously associated only with, say, forestland, and not with high desert like this."

I met Bob at his lonely post, some 50 miles north of the New Mexico border and midway between the Centennial State's eastern and western boundaries. Here, in the crook of a bend in the Sangre de Cristo Mountains, lie the tallest inland sand dunes in North America—great dun-colored waves cresting 700 feet above the windswept greasewood plain of the San Luis Valley. "People are as fascinated by the dunes as they are by geysers," he said. "You wouldn't expect to find 150 square miles of sand dunes 8,200 feet up in the Rockies, would you?"

Neither did Zebulon Pike, the first American explorer to see them. Sent by the government to explore the southwestern lands of the Louisiana Purchase, Pike struggled down from the snow-covered Sangre de Cristos in 1807 with ten hungry, frostbitten men, only to encounter these new obstacles. "Their appearance," he later wrote, "was exactly that of a sea in a storm." To me, they looked as though the Sahara had advanced to the base of the Alps.

"Sometimes the dunes are pink, sometimes gray. They can be red, gold, white—even blue. Depends on the light and the season and the time of day." Berle Lewis peered out the window of the Zapata Ranch's log-built workshop to check the current hue. "Sort of tan right now. That's about usual." A quick, bright-eyed septuagenarian ranch hand, Berle lives with his wife in a 120-year-old log and adobe house that originally served as a stagecoach stop. I caught him hard at work building feed and salt boxes for the ranch's 2,000 head of cattle. "The dunes are full of surprises," he said, sighting along a board he intended to saw. "Wind still uncovers Indian fire rings from the early 1800s. Charcoal, animal bones, that kind of thing."

Archaeologists have found 11,500-year-old stone spearpoints in the dunes, weapons used to kill the mammoths, early bison, and giant wolves that roamed the ancient plain. They have identified 10,000-year-old campsites just south of the sand hills. From this and other evidence, geologists believe the dunes began to form at least 12,000 years ago as the last ice age ended. Back then the Rio Grande flowed east from the San Juan Mountains across the valley, turning southward where the windward fringe of the sand sea lies today. With time the river moved south, leaving a broad floodplain. Scoured by prevailing southwesterlies and replenished by erosion from the San Juans, this alluvial basin provides an inexhaustible supply of sand.

"Because of the prevailing wind, the dunes are usually advancing northeast, toward the Sangre de Cristos," explained Bob Schultz. "But Medano Creek blocks the way and washes sand back south into the valley. There the southwesterlies pick it up again and blow it back into the dunes. Opposing storm winds from the mountains then pile the sand on itself, which is why the dunes get so high. All these forces keep the dunes on a geologic treadmill. Photos taken 40 years ago show they haven't changed much."

Nevertheless, standing in the rippled troughs between these mammoth dunes often gave me an eerie sensation of arrested motion, as though the sand waves looming above were about to curl over and break against the flank of the Sangre de Cristos, swallowing me forever. The experience is common to visitors, and probably explains why the August 6, 1885, issue of the *Alamosa Journal* gave credence to a wandering Mexican's tale that 3,500 of his grandfather's sheep vanished here in 1816, swallowed up in a terrific windstorm along with four herders and their cabins and corrals. "I don't buy that one," said Bob. "We have 'avalanches' all the time out there. Some of them might be an inch and a half deep. If you stood still for 30 years, you just might be covered."

"I kind of liked the Mexican's story," said old-time rancher Howard Shockey, whose living room window frames an unobstructed view of 14,345-foot Blanca Peak, 25 miles distant across the uninhabited plain, and the highest in the Sangre de Cristos. "Folks here enjoy a good yarn. They'd rather believe it than the truth."

Opened to homesteading in 1862, the San Luis Valley was quickly staked out by Mexican ranchers, followed by Mormon farming clans and others. Starting with those Victorian-era settlers, the dunes became a favorite picnic spot for valley residents. Howard showed me an old album filled with fading photographs of Gibson girl look-alikes on ponies. One snapshot commemorated "Our ride across the Sand." A frequent destination was the gold-mining settlement of Liberty.

Toward the end of my sojourn I camped not far from there for several days, along the eastern edge of the sand, where Castle Creek flows into the Medano. Late one afternoon, after a hike deep into the dunes, I sat by the entrance of my tent and brewed a cup of tea. To the north, a storm advanced on lightning-bolt legs over the 20-million-year-old steeples of the Sangre de Cristos, wreathing the snowcapped peaks in dark clouds beneath a clear blue sky.

There might have been a road past my camp had Liberty not gone bust. The ore ran out around the turn of the century, and today only a few log buildings remain. "They'd take out $75,000, then spend $150,000 tryin' to find more," Howard had told me. "I think gold fever got 'em." Perhaps. I suspect it's also possible their optimism may have sprung from rapture inspired by the beauties of this place. They might have been seduced by the ever changing hues of the high desert palette, as rich as any fabled El Dorado. If so, I understood the seduction.

By the time my explorations of the Rocky Mountain states led me to the Colorado Plateau, I had begun to wonder how words could do justice to the myriad beauties I had seen. The moment I first looked out across southeastern Utah's Canyonlands National Park, I knew why Freeman Tilden called this "the place where the adjective died from exhaustion."

Canyonlands is a 527-square-mile wilderness of sedimentary rock, sculpted by wind, rain, ice, and the flow of the Green and Colorado Rivers into an unimaginably complex labyrinth of mesas, buttes, chasms, spires, arches, and balanced rock formations. I had my first look from Island in the Sky mesa, where Grand View Point Overlook (the park's best vantage point) gives a 6,080-foot-high perspective on the distant Abajo and Henry Mountains. Converging in the park's midsection, the Green and the Colorado form a Y, dividing Canyonlands into three distinct sections. In its northern crook lies Island in the Sky, with The Maze to the west of the rivers, and The Needles to the south and east.

"You won't find more difficult terrain anywhere," said Jerry Rumburg, chief interpreter at the Park Service's Canyonlands headquarters in Moab, where I stopped to pick up a backcountry permit. He listed the things I should think about. "Few roads, no water, no services. No phones, ranches, ranger stations. Nothing. You'd better be well prepared before you venture there."

Small hardships in view of the riches within. Below the confluence of the Green and the Colorado lies Cataract Canyon, a 1,500-foot-deep chasm that rumbles with some of the country's most challenging white water. To the west of the Green the zigzag canyons of The Maze offer a 119-square-mile hiker's dream—or nightmare—so difficult to reach it remains one of our least-visited parklands. Here and in The Needles are some of the finest examples of prehistoric rock art on the continent. Throughout Canyonlands, nestled under cliff overhangs and poised atop mesas, are the stone and mud ruins of dwellings, storehouses, and granaries left by the vanished Anasazi, believed to be ancestors of the Southwest's Pueblo tribes. And everywhere "the splendor of the landscape," writes Edward Abbey, "the perfection of the silence. . . ."

Eighteenth-century Spanish explorations of the Southwest probed Utah's southernmost canyonlands but did not reach inside today's park boundaries. The first European known to have visited was a French trapper named Denis Julien, who ventured here in 1836. When Americans arrived in the summer of 1859, their map showed the plateau as a blank below the heading, "Region Unexplored Scientifically."

"Long as I can remember back, there was *nobody* out there 'cept'n cowhands and gold hunters," Earl LaMotte told me. An itinerant cowhand most of his 71 working years ("started scrubbin' pots on a Montana chuck wagon when I was 13, retired my 85th birthday"), Earl is 94 and lives in a trailer home near Mexican Hat. Short, bowlegged and lean, hands and face tanned by the high desert sun, he settled into his recliner and reminisced about punching cattle in The Needles.

"Used to give me the heebie-jeebies at first, workin' up there. You was always dead-endin', lookin' straight down or straight up, stock thirsty and you rimrocked a hundred feet above water. Up around Salt Creek there was Indian pictures, spooky faces and handprints, bright as though they was painted yesterday. Ruins up in Horse Canyon got me to thinkin' they was still around, hidin', watchin' me.

"Nights, moon come up, coyotes start a hollerin'. Needles cut a shadow looked like a bunch of guys standin' at the foot of your bedroll. Wasn't until the '50s we got any folks at all out here, runnin' around in Jeeps with Geiger counters, lathered up with uranium fever. That petered out, though, and they scattered. It's hard country, all right. Only thing has it easy in there is the rivers."

Earl's remark raised a key point about Canyonlands. Though trails and primitive roads let me drive and hike parts of the interior, I could not escape a sense of restriction: There is no overland route crossing the entire park. The zigzag canyons of The Maze are barely ten air miles from Island in the Sky's Grand View Point, yet I had to drive a roundabout loop of 200 miles to reach them. I decided to take to the rivers.

The Colorado enters canyonland country near Moab, through a breach in an 800-foot-high cliff known as The Portal. From there the silty ocher river follows a placid course, dropping barely one foot per mile and entering the park some 33 river miles downstream. From the Canyonlands boundary it is another 30 miles to the mouth of the Green. Four miles beyond, the Colorado accelerates, dropping more than ten feet per mile as it tumbles over 28 rapids in 16-mile-long Cataract Canyon before leveling out in the still waters of Lake Powell in the Glen Canyon National Recreation Area.

*In all seasons trust Old
Faithful; in winter,
Yellowstone's showstopper
puts on an unusual
display. The anvil head
of water vapor typifies
a deep-freeze dawn, when
dense cold air sinks low in
the geyser basin, creating
a temperature inversion.
Cooling swiftly as it
rises, the vapor soon hits
warmer, lighter air—and
flattens out. Old Faithful
spouts off 20 times each
day; of the millions who
view it every year, only
one in 20 sees the winter
spectacle. PAGES 126-127:
Above the park's volcanic
boilers simmer 10,000
thermal features, including
the mud pots, hot springs,
and fumaroles steaming
beyond the rim of the
Grand Canyon of
the Yellowstone River.*

I decided to put my canoe into the Green near the park's north-western corner and join the Colorado at the confluence. With a week's supply of food sealed up in three watertight bags, ten gallons of drinking water in two rubber jerricans, and a friend to return my truck to Moab, I headed south on the Island in the Sky road through a spring shower. Turning west off the pavement onto dirt, I shifted into four-wheel drive and bounced across Horsethief Point, a plateau covered with 180-million-year-old rock and softened by Utah juniper, piñon pine, blackbrush, shad scale, yucca, rabbitbrush, greasewood, sage, and flow-ering ephedra bushes.

Arriving at the Mineral Bottom put-in some 1,400 feet below the mesa top, we lowered the canoe onto Mesozoic era rocks 225 million years old. It was noon before my gear was stowed. The truck's departure left me in that profound stillness that attests to wilderness. Life jacket strapped on, I walked the canoe out into the river, stepped in, and shoved off. The current pulled me along at the pace of a museum stroll.

Through the day I paddled only to keep the bow pointed down-stream. With afternoon the canyon fell into shadow. Swallows dove at me from the cliffs, let out sharp cries, and cannonballed downriver. That evening I made camp on the sand dunes of Saddle Horse Bottom. At dusk I brewed coffee over a gas stove as kangaroo rats and piñon mice chattered in the brush. Shadows lengthened; the canyon rim flared red, then lavender, mauve, gunmetal blue, and purple. The moon rose full, and somewhere a coyote yelped, soon joined by others.

The following day the river bottom broadened, and the banks and sand flats grew thick with cottonwood, tamarisk, and willow—shelter for deer, fox, beaver, bobcats, and migratory birds. After floating about seven miles, I beached the canoe at Fort Bottom to explore a pair of two-story circular towers rising on a bluff amidst collapsed ruins, evidence of the vanished Anasazi. As far back as a thousand years ago, the Anasazi had farmed here, apparently abandoning the area for the Arizona region in the 13th century after years of a killing drought.

Four more days of drifting and exploring brought me to the conflu-ence, in all a peaceful journey of 50 miles. I pulled the canoe onto a sandbar to watch the rust-red water of the Colorado run parallel with the blue-tinged Green until the latter tapered away. From here on to the Sea of Cortez, where 300 million years of silt deposits commemorate the Southwest's canyon country, the fabled red river takes command.

After floating the Green and the Colorado Rivers in 1909, industrialist-adventurer Julius Stone remembered his emotions as he ap-proached the confluence. "The scene is hard, weird, and fascinating in its strangeness," he wrote. "It stimulates the observer in a strange way. He is tempted to exertion beyond his strength. He must needs see what is beyond, and then what is still beyond." In the seven months since my first step into the Bitterroots 600 miles north, I had learned that the temptation Stone felt is not to be resisted. That knowledge, to me, was the Rocky Mountains' greatest gift.

STEVEN FULLER

F*ed by thermal waters, the ice-free Madison River makes inviting habitats for the winter crowd at Yellowstone. Canada geese go with the flow as a young cow elk watches. The female red fox below spent the season with a male near the lower falls of the Yellowstone—the first red foxes to winter there in at least 13 years, according to park observers.*

Grain by grain, the grit of mountain and floodplain flies on the winds— the parched treasure of Great Sand Dunes National Monument in Colorado. Winds crest the dunes, ripple them, reverse them. A visitor, above, runs down a dune face; some even schuss down on skis. No harm—wind soon erases all tracks. The dunes seem to change colors: A low sun can set them aflame, along with the Sangre de Cristo Mountains that confine the sand hills. PAGES 132-133: Wind brings seeds; finding moisture, they blossom forth, as do these pioneering sunflowers near Medano Creek. When the wind brings more sand, it may bury the flowers.

THE SOUTHWEST

Where Rainbows Wait for the Rain

TOM ALGIRE

R ealm of grandeur, the arid Southwest enfolds a land of eroded canyons, mesas, mountains, and caverns. Exemplifying the contradictory appeal of this sere region, vibrant blossoms of prickly pear cactus (above) emerge from a forbidding barrier of thorns. At sunset, muted colors soften the edges of the South Rim of the Grand Canyon in northern Arizona (opposite). In evening's clear light, autumn-tinged shrubs glow along the canyon's North Rim (pages 136-137). Noted British writer J.B. Priestley likened this most sublime gorge to "all Beethoven's nine symphonies in stone and magic light."

TOM ALGIRE

THE SOUTHWEST

By Jennifer C. Urquhart

From the yawning breach of the Grand Canyon to the fantastic interior worlds of New Mexico's Carlsbad Caverns, America's Southwest offers a window on enchantment. Vistas here stretch to the horizon across rainbow-hued badlands and fossilized forest remnants in Arizona's Painted Desert. They extend over the mountain reaches of west Texas—to the volcano-formed Chisos, the massive Guadalupe escarpment, and the history-rich Davis Mountains.

Perhaps it comes in the clear air, or in the great thunderheads that pass over in the afternoons, sprinkling a few drops of rain like holy water on the sere ground. It may be in mirages that shimmer across a road at high noon, teasing with visions of lakes and castles. Or is it in the sense of limitless space, where the bare bones of the earth's form lie exposed, unsoftened by cloak of forest or grass? Whether it be in Arizona's red rock country or in the vast rangeland of west Texas, the arid Southwest casts its own special spell.

Today the region intrigues, draws people. It has not always been so. Americans were late to appreciate its stark beauty. From the Spanish on, early explorers found the region at the very least unappealing and home to strange plants and creatures, and more often a harsh, alien emptiness known as the Great American Desert. Certainly not beautiful. Probing the area in the spring of 1858, U.S. Army Lt. Joseph C. Ives wrote the region off as "altogether valueless. . . . Ours has been the first, and will doubtless be the last, party of whites to visit this profitless locality. . . . intended by nature [to] be forever unvisited and undisturbed."

But only a few short decades after the Ives expedition visitors began to flock to the desert Southwest. And the Grand Canyon of the Colorado River had become, in the words of Teddy Roosevelt, "the one great sight which every American . . . should see." Even Lieutenant Ives knew the "Big Cañon" was "unrivalled in grandeur." But wouldn't Ives be surprised to see the countless vehicles that cruise the South Rim today, and the throngs at Mather and Hopi Points, cameras at the ready to capture sunset over the canyon.

If they can. "At first glance the spectacle seems too strange to be real," writes one naturalist. "It stuns the eye but cannot really hold the attention. . . . the scale is too large to be credited." The Grand Canyon demands perception in stages. And so it was for me on my first visit, at age 11, to the Southwest and to the canyon. Memories of that trip center mostly on a well-trained, placid mule named Elsie who carried me down a worn trail into the canyon. So enthralled was I with Elsie that I was nearly oblivious of the vertical plunges at trail's edge, and, for the most part, of the geological spectacle that unfolded before me. In later years I found a different view of the great gorge. From a rubber raft on the mud-laden waters of the Colorado, a mile below the rim, I craned up at the dark, looming Vishnu Schist in the Inner Gorge. These rocks, oldest in the canyon, were formed perhaps two billion years ago.

This time my first glimpse of the canyon came just after sunset. I stepped away from people on the South Rim and moved closer to the edge. It was as if the bottom of the world had simply dropped away into an immense void before me. Buttes, mesas, escarpments, buttresses, chasms—veiled in evening shades of blue and violet—marched to the horizon, offering no clue to establish scale. All chatter and babble of voices behind me, even my own heartbeat, vanished in an engulfing silence and calmness.

If the Grand Canyon will set no scale for itself, it offers perspective

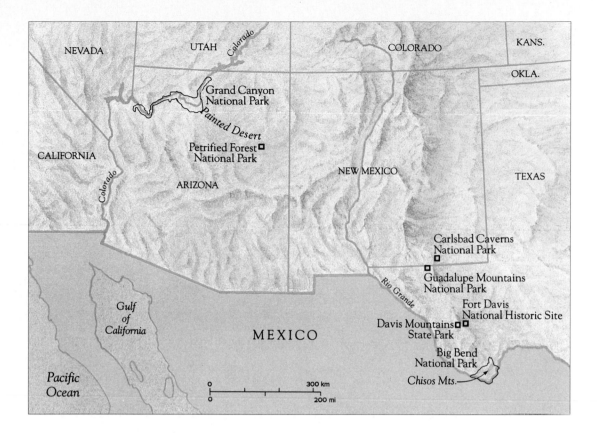

on man and his small instant on this planet. All the exotic names bestowed on the canyon formations—a panoply of deities: Brahma, Jupiter, Isis, Shiva, Wotan—become inadequate, and mere dimensions—that the canyon is up to 18 miles wide and 227 miles long—meaningless.

"Every time you see it, it's different," said Eunice Ganteaume. A native New Yorker, Eunice lives in Prescott and has adapted happily to the Southwest. "There are only two ways to go around here—up and down!" At that moment we were going down the Grandview Trail, still ice-covered near the rim from a late winter storm. I picked my way carefully, bracing on a ski pole to keep from catapulting into space off the steep switchback trail. I had joined Eunice and her husband, George Ruffner, for a hike to some old copper mines on Horseshoe Mesa. It was early March, and snow still lay in mounds in shaded corners. But even at this time of year, we each carried half a gallon of water and had cached some under an old juniper by the trail for the return trip.

"It's really hard to pack in this place," said George, who is a biologist. "It may be 24°F at the rim and 80° at the bottom." We slowly made our way beyond the icy stretches and down steep cliffs where steps had been constructed using stones and timber.

"Somethin' sure happened here," the old cowboy is supposed to have said, at first sight of the Grand Canyon. And he was right.

"Kissing takes concentration; however, some requires more breathing than others," said George.

"What?" I said. George had my undivided attention. "That phrase is one way to remember the canyon's major geological formations," he said. "The first letter in each word corresponds to one of the formations." He began listing the colorful rock layers like old friends, going back in time from the most recent: the tan Kaibab Limestone, light-colored Toroweap and Coconino, bright red Hermit Shale, light red Supai, Redwall Limestone, grayish green Muav Limestone and Bright Angel Shale, mottled Tapeats Sandstone; "others" in George's catch-phrase includes the oldest formations at the bottom of the canyon.

Each layer of rock remains as evidence of the endless process that has created the Grand Canyon and is still shaping it: the eons of limestone and sandstone building up, then wearing away again; of deserts invading and retreating; of winds and water, armed with particles of sand and silt, carving through rock layers; of volcanic outbursts and tectonic upheavals.

We relaxed at lunch near the old mines. Now only rusting mining equipment and crumbling structures remain, and scattered bits of blue-green copper ore. In the 1890s mules packed the ore—200 pounds each—up the trail we had hiked down. Before long the miners discovered tourists were more profitable, and a hotel was opened near the rim.

"The light has changed so much," said Eunice as we started back up the trail. Harsh reds and yellows had given way to pinks and purples. In the hot sun the snow at the rim looked inviting. Ravens floated on thermals; their harsh cries seemed to taunt us who are bound to earth.

On other days I tried different trails into the canyon. Always it is the formidable cliffs of the Redwall that present the most unbroken barrier. "I'm just in love with the Redwall," said Laurie Francom, a fellow hiker from California. We were headed to Phantom Ranch at the bottom of the gorge. "It's the *key*," she said. "If you can find a way down the Redwall, you can find a way down into the canyon." The Redwall limestone is actually a dull gray. Its red color comes from iron oxide that has washed down from the Hermit and Supai formations above.

On the Bright Angel Trail we traversed the Redwall easily in a series of switchbacks known as Jacob's Ladder. It was a different story on the South Kaibab Trail the next morning. Up and up we trudged on an endless series of switchbacks hacked into the limestone wall. Finally we leveled off on the top of the Redwall along an exposed ridge where junipers and pines clung. Agave stalks, dead and blown over, lay scattered. From atop the rocky spine, ridges and mesas and side canyons extended as far as I could see—almost like a dare. Though I visited this "most sublime spectacle in nature" a hundred times or a thousand, I could never tire of the Grand Canyon, and there would always be new trails to follow to new corners of beauty and solitude.

I headed southeast from the Grand Canyon across the northern Arizona plateau. Light and shadow in a squally sky played across soft reds, blues, and yellows of a rainbow landscape known as the Painted Desert. Drifting rain turned to gold in errant shafts of sunlight.

If the Grand Canyon paints in brash, spectacular strokes two billion years of the earth's story, the Painted Desert renders in colors just as vivid a more detailed view. My destination was the Petrified Forest, an hourglass-shaped national park on the edge of the Painted Desert.

At first glance, the area seems to visitors a colorful wasteland, "where even jackrabbits and snakes would find it hard to survive," park superintendent Ed Gastellum said. "But we are just at the tip of the iceberg in uncovering the story here. There isn't any place in the world, scientists say, that has as complete a story as we are able to tell here—of the relationship of plants and animals in an upland environment during the Triassic period, about 230 million years ago." Ed is excited about all the new discoveries. "Until 1980 we knew of only five species of vertebrates here. Now we know of about 40, and over 200 fossil plants."

Petrified Forest National Park was established originally to protect logs and tree stumps fossilized more than 200 million years ago under layers of sediment. Now new discoveries of other plant and animal fossils have greatly broadened the goals of the 147-square-mile park. The aim is to present a picture of that long-ago world, when the whole region was warmer and wetter. "Try to visualize what it was like then," said Ed: "Tropical, with rivers and streams. No birds, mammals, flowering plants or grasses, no butterflies."

We headed out to look at some of the well-known areas of the park, Jasper Forest, Agate Bridge, Rainbow Forest, Crystal Forest. For it is the jewel-like fossil wood of every hue—transformed as if by a "sea-change," in Shakespeare's words, "Into something rich and strange"—that brings most visitors here. Water did play its part. Logs from ancient forests washed onto a floodplain in the late Triassic period. Then, many times, floods covered the area, receded again, and added layer upon layer of sediment over the logs. Rather than disintegrating, the logs were preserved, cell by cell, as silica replaced organic matter.

"Erosion, that's what this place is all about," said Ed. For eventually the layers of sediment eroded away, exposing the fossilized logs. Erosion also shaped the striated moonscape we looked out on. "This is Blue Mesa—one of my favorite areas because of the banding of color," said Ed. "Especially at sunrise or sunset. You kind of wonder what it was like when this was first being discovered by Europeans, or by the Indians for that matter. What were their impressions?"

For the Navajo the fossil logs were bones of the "Great Giant." The Paiutes believed they were the arrow shafts of their thunder god, Shinuav. Such sacred connections, however, did not stop Native Americans from utilizing fossil wood for building. Or from incising hundreds of petroglyphs into the dark patina of rock faces all over the area. Ed showed me some of these. At one place we must have walked a mile past a jumble of boulders etched like billboards along an ancient highway, with every imaginable design. Were they simple doodling, or was it art, or symbols of cosmic significance? No one knows. Some, experts are certain, relate closely to solar equinoxes.

"The Dinosaur/A Beast of Yore/Doesn't Live Here/Anymore," read the verse on the front door of the Gastellums' house. It was carefully lettered by Jana Gastellum, age seven, one of Ed's daughters, and quite correct, too. But one dinosaur is causing a lively stir these days here in the park. Her name is "Gertie," and "she" was unearthed in 1984 by paleontologist Rob Long. "I wish we had a better name for it," said Ed, "but we won't until Rob's research paper is completed. He took the name Gertie from a 1912 cartoon." In reality, there's no reason to assume that the dinosaur was female. And the bones were actually from several animals.

What is important about Gertie is that one of the specimens in the group of bones dug up may be the oldest articulated dinosaur fossil ever found in a location that can be dated. And it may prove to be the link between earlier animals in this region and the later dinosaurs.

But Gertie, or at least her bones, have gone off to the University of California at Berkeley to be studied. I had to settle for a crocodile-like phytosaur. We were a crew of ten on a Saturday morning standing on a steep, windswept ridge to the west of park headquarters. Ed, his wife, Carolyn, and several specialists and volunteers worked under the direction of paleontologist Dr. David Gillette of the New Mexico Museum of Natural History. After portable jackhammers had blasted away overburden, we used shovels, brooms, trowels, our hands to scrabble away dirt and debris. Huge vertebrae emerged out of the hillside, then a bottom jaw, twisted in an odd, agonized angle.

To think that a creature that lived 225 million years ago was coming out of a barren Arizona hillside before our eyes. "And to think we are the first to see it," said Carolyn Gastellum. "Every time I'm out here, I just wonder what else lies in here."

The phytosaur had been discovered and partially excavated the previous summer. We were continuing the dig. A stocky man in his late thirties, Dave Gillette leaned on his shovel and told me a little about the animal we were uncovering. "We're into rocks 225 million years old, a time of transition when the dinosaurs were coming on. The phytosaurs were dominant when the dinosaur emerged," he said. "What's fascinating is why animals that were adapted to this terrain lost out to the dinosaurs. It's a matter of speculation why they vanished."

And how big was our phytosaur? "You know, we never found the end of it last summer, Dave," said one of the crew. "Probably about 25 feet long, weighing a ton or so," Dave replied. Formidable, too. It probably ate the likes of Gertie, only about a third its size.

Late one afternoon I hiked alone toward the Black Forest region in the northern end of the park. I crossed the wide area known as the Lithodendron Wash. Faraway ridges, tinted in pastel colors, edged the horizon. Bits of petrified wood were strewn on the ground. Tiny saltbush plants, like porcelain roses, had taken on a magenta blush. Fast-moving clouds, bright white and dark, gave definition to the expanse. On the other side of the wash I sat among the glistening, manganese-stained stone logs of the Black Forest. Many were in neat fireplace lengths, as if prepared for winter by some ancient Paul Bunyan. There was no sound except a gentle wind rattling dried seed pods in the grass.

I n contrast to the vivid red rock canyons and banded badlands of northern Arizona, the mountains of west Texas float in the ethereal shades of a dream. That softness is deceptive, for these mountains offer a no less rugged terrain. Indian legend has it that when the Creator had finished making the earth and the heavens, he had a lot of stony material left over. He just tossed it away into one big heap that is mountainous west Texas—Big Bend country.

Early Spanish explorers called it *El Despoblado*—the uninhabited land. Even so a kind of cultural crossroads grew here, a blend of Indian, Spanish, Mexican, and Anglo-European in a rich cultural legacy. It is a natural crossroads, too, where the parched Chihuahuan Desert meets upland forests and lush, spring-fed glades.

My first glimpse of Texas's western mountains was of the Guadalupes, in the far northwestern part of the state. I had headed east from El Paso, across salt flats, and across rangeland dotted with mesquite and bronzy-green creosote. Every now and then came a cluster of derelict buildings or the bright red of a Chevron sign glaring against the pale landscape. And finally, ahead loomed the massive escarpment called El Capitan, the southernmost peak of the Guadalupe Mountains.

"I've often pondered whether people driving by ever wonder why this was made into a park," said the park's manager, Ralph Harris, who knows plenty of reasons why this area at the tail end of the Rockies was designated Guadalupe Mountains National Park. He would show me some of them. From the road, the massif looks forbidding, impenetrable—and windy. " 'Does the wind always blow this way?' visitors invariably ask," said Ralph. "I tell them, 'No, it sometimes blows the other way!' " It was windy enough at park headquarters that a gust snatched a postcard, all written and stamped, out of my hand and sent it airmail forever across the cactus-studded expanse. "Used to have barbed wire," an old cowhand told me, "but the wind blowed the barbs clean off."

Two hundred fifty million years ago all this was ocean reef at the edge of the Permian Sea. Primitive plants and animals—mainly algae and sponges—died, collected on the ocean floor, and built the reef. The ocean receded, and the land was tilted upward to form the mountain range. "I fantasize about scuba diving around this ancient reef," said Ralph. "Hope you are a good swimmer," the ruddy-faced veteran ranger added. We had driven to the western side of the park to check a remote rain station and to see some gypsum dunes. No rain this month. Today we would have to settle for a dry view of *(Continued on page 150)*

Yard-thick fossil logs lie in Petrified Forest National Park. Some 200 million years ago, lush jungle grew here. As trees fell, flooding streams buried them under silt and mud. Gradually silica replaced organic tissue. Later, wind and water uncovered the logs. A gleaming slab of polished fossil wood (opposite) shows traces of iron in tints of yellow and orange. Moonrise meets sunset (pages 146-147) over banded cliffs of the Painted Desert.

*M*onumental or as delicate as lace, the features of the Big Room at Carlsbad Caverns awe visitors. Over millennia, drop by drop, limestone-bearing water has created an infinite variety of forms in this national park's 72 caves. Largest chamber of all, the Big Room equals 11 football fields in area.

the ancient limestone reef, and, for surf, we would have to make do with sand. I took the plunge. Flour-fine sand whipped in rooster tails from the crest of the dune. Silken particles of the whitest white flowed like water between my toes as I slid 40 or 50 feet down. Trails opened behind my feet and closed as quickly, leaving not a trace. Again and again we ran up the sloping windward side of another dune, then leapt off the edge. We chased a spiny lizard, caught up with it. As it froze in place, Ralph stroked its head. It took off in an awkward, long-legged run. "These dunes are moving east toward the mountains—a grain at a time," said Ralph. They are now outside the park, though there's a move to include them. Meanwhile, they may just take themselves there on their own.

For Wallace E. Pratt, a New York geologist who in the 1920s explored for oil in this parched land, one lush corner of the Guadalupes was the "most beautiful spot in Texas." McKittrick Canyon. Pratt soon bought the land, and in 1957 he donated 5,632 acres to the federal government. It would become the nucleus of the park—its northeastern portion—and one of its most favored areas.

A surprising range of vegetation grows in well-watered and sheltered McKittrick. Ralph Harris and I started up the dry creek bed. "Where else can you stand and look at prickly pear, ponderosas, maples, live oaks, chinquapins, madrones?" said Ralph. In the Chihuahuan Desert, "each plant . . . is a porcupine," a 19th-century traveler wrote. "It is nature armed to the teeth." The awkward-limbed cholla cactus is no exception. "This one's called 'jumping cactus,'" said Ralph, "because it seems to leap out and catch your clothes from several feet away." Sharp blades of sotol, agave, yucca, bristled at our ankles and knees. "They're real friendly compared to the catclaw acacia." The demeanor of the madrone is more refined. Strips of reddish bark peel away to reveal the silken inner bark that earns the tree the name lady's leg. A whiptail lizard scurried by. "They have an odd survival adaptation," said Ralph. "They have no males—only females. Hope that never catches on!"

Farther up the canyon we came to the hardwoods McKittrick is known for. The trees here seemed small. And, like giants in Lilliput land, we wandered through groves of diminutive maples, oaks with tiny acorns, ash, walnut, chinquapin, all more familiar in the East than in west Texas. "The fall color is spectacular," said Ralph. In odd contrast to this elfin forest were the agaves, with their 15-foot stalks like huge asparagus for one of Gulliver's Brobdingnagians. In one grand display, before withering and dying, these stalks would open into full candelabra of golden blossoms. Called mescal by the Apaches who lived in this area, agaves were an important source of food, fiber—and a potent liquor— hence the name Mescalero Apache.

High above this small canyon, in another area of the park, I would find vegetation even more surprising for the desert. "In effect," said park naturalist Bob Valen, "if this were on the flat, we would have to travel more than a thousand miles north to equal the vegetation change we experience here by climbing 2,000 feet."

Under a beating sun we scrambled up a steep, rocky trail. "This is called Bear Canyon Trail—and it's a bear!" said Bob. Often we stopped to gulp some water in the shade of a gnarled juniper or small oak or maple. At last we reached the Bowl, a shallow depression atop the Guadalupe massif and more than 8,000 feet high. A forest of conifers—Douglas fir, ponderosa and limber pines—and aspens survives here, a relict of the last ice age, when such plants spread southward. We sat in a cool, breezy glade, very different from the desert 2,000 feet below. A little higher up, atop 8,366-foot Hunter Peak, we braced ourselves against a buffeting wind and looked across to the bare limestone ramparts of Guadalupe Peak, at 8,749 feet the highest point in Texas. To the south stretched the high Texas prairie, unrelieved to the horizon.

It takes only a few hot, desiccated days in this region's relentless wind to appreciate what a pocket of forest or a little spring-fed verdure can mean to people here. Or, for that matter, the subterranean world of a cave. "In summer, a lot of local senior citizens come here several times a week just to cool off and walk a little," a staff member told me at Carlsbad Caverns National Park just across the New Mexico state line from Guadalupe. "The cave stays a steady 56°F year-round." An appealing thought, as I left blinding noonday sun for the twilight zone a few hundred yards inside Carlsbad Cavern, largest of 72 caves in the park. A few swallows and an early rising bat or two flitted aloft. By sunset thousands of the flying mammals would burst forth to feed on insects.

Soon I was deep inside the ancient Capitan Reef, where so recently I had hiked to the top. And I was cool. Geologically speaking, Carlsbad and the Guadalupe Mountains are flip sides of the same formation. Over millions of years, water, slightly acidic after percolating downward through the soil here, had dissolved yawning interior spaces in the reef limestone. The reef then rose above sea level, and air replaced water in these spaces. Mineral-rich water, endlessly dripping, began the job of decorating the caves, creating stalagmites rising from the floor, stalactites hanging from the ceiling, taking every possible form.

Round and round I circled, ever downward hundreds of feet into the cave, past columns, translucent draperies, lacy stone waterfalls as thin as hair, chandeliers, and whimsical characters out of a Grimm's fairy-tale world. Names of rooms and formations teased the imagination: Whale's Mouth, Papoose Room, Bashful Elephant, Queen's Chamber. Finally I reached the Big Room. Covering some 12 acres and rising to 285 feet in places, it seemed to be a great cathedral inhabited by enchanted beings forever frozen in attitudes of calm meditation.

El Capitan retreated in my rearview mirror as I turned back into Texas toward the Davis Mountains. Afternoon shadows crept across the road. Tumbleweeds followed and gathered along fences. Doves and mockingbirds flew up in waves. A roadrunner preferred a footrace.

Mirage lakes tantalized ahead. It was dry this day, but sometimes that water must be real. Signs at deep dips in the road warn about flash flooding. Their gauges register to five feet.

These mountains look different from the flat-topped Guadalupes. Abruptly rising peaks and rugged outcroppings, from volcanic upheavals some 50 million years ago, rise out of hilly ranch country. Bunches of grass shimmered in the evening light. Dozens of pronghorns browsed among the herds of Herefords and crossbred cattle.

"The Davis Mountains are a sort of oasis," a local rancher told me soon after I arrived. "This is volcanic country—lava rocks underlie a water table and natural springs." These mountains form a kind of oasis, too, for Texans from the hot, featureless prairie to the east. They come to Davis Mountains State Park, a tiny reserve tucked away in Limpia Canyon, and to the Fort Davis National Historic Site—and to the little town of Fort Davis itself.

"I don't think there's anywhere as nice as Fort Davis," said Pansy Espy, a rancher's wife, avid bird-watcher, and history buff. The town does have charm, in its forthright, turn-of-the-century buildings and the cupola-crowned courthouse set among spreading shade trees in a carefully nurtured lawn. Turnstiles once kept out any stray livestock without court business. People here like to tell how they happen to have the good fortune to live in Fort Davis: "Papa was given the job of driving a herd of cattle here in 1885," said 93-year-old Jessie Jones Mueller. Another person's grandfather opened the mercantile store.

Pansy's grandfather was a Texas Ranger. An energetic, bespectacled woman in her late sixties, Pansy had pulled up in her old Lincoln at the local historical society. Soon we were rummaging among relics and memorabilia: saddles, barber chairs, churns, cider presses, branding irons, barbed wire, boots—and dust, lots of dust. Piles of heavy wool quilts were stacked in one corner. "Old Nick Mersfelder, who owned this place, rented those to cowboys for a dollar a night. They'd come into town on Saturday, take a bath in his old tin tub, go to the dance. Then they'd come back here and wrap up in a quilt to sleep," Pansy said.

"Fort Davis wouldn't be anything without the old fort," Pansy told me. Early one morning I climbed a steep trail from Davis Mountains State Park, then followed a level volcanic ridge. Chollas bloomed bright magenta-purple. Spiky sotol and a large yucca called Spanish dagger dotted slopes below me. Eventually I looked down into a shallow box canyon and at its mouth spread Fort Davis. Veranda-shaded bungalows that once housed officers and their families edged one side of a broad parade ground, long barracks for enlisted men the other.

A melancholy bugle call wafted up to me from the empty field, a ghostly reminder of bustling cavalry and marching soldiers of long ago. From 1854 to 1891—except for the Civil War years—Fort Davis was a key outpost in defense of settlers, travelers, and the mail on the route to El Paso, against the Apache and Comanche. A peek through a window of one house revealed a Victorian damask-and-walnut elegance I found surprising for the wilds of the 1880s West. Just by chance at Fort Davis, I would stumble across a little of my own family history. It was an offhand question when I asked park superintendent Douglas C. McChristian if I might be able to find out if my mother's grandfather had ever been at the fort. He had, I knew, served in the Army in the West after the Civil War, but that's about all I knew. It took a bit of poking around in the park's library, but suddenly there he was—the archival record showed, in a spidery hand, R. G. Heiner, Captain, First Infantry, Company A. He had been assigned to Fort Davis for a few months in 1881 to serve on a court-martial.

"There's a black connection here at the fort that surprises visitors," said Doug McChristian. "We are one of a handful of forts to have had all four post-Civil War black regiments here at one time or another." These regiments of "Buffalo Soldiers"—the Indians' name for them—served in campaigns all over the West and achieved a "notable record of military accomplishment." Now the fort, which became a national historic site in 1961, highlights that important aspect of its history.

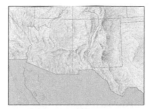

I continued my journey south to Big Bend National Park, where I'd be looking not for my great-grandfather, but for a rainbow. "The place where the rainbows wait for the rain," an old Mexican vaquero—or cowboy—called Big Bend country, "and the big river is kept in a stone box. . . . and the mountains float in the air. . . ."

The geology here is complex, experts concede, "strangely mixed," tilted, folded, stood on end, turned upside down, and generally jumbled by volcanic catastrophe. "Wildly weird"—so one 1895 visitor described the country. Since 1944, an 1,100-square-mile national park has encompassed this isolated part of west Texas. It is not on the way to anywhere. "You've got to be really wanting to come here to visit Big Bend," one park ranger told me. Its remoteness pleases some. "I reckon the best thing about this part of Texas," said one old-timer, "is that it's lonesomer than any place else."

Here the Rio Grande makes a sweeping turn northeast and carves through mountains to create canyons more than a thousand feet deep— the vaquero's stone box. From a distance as I approached, the Chisos Mountains floated on airy vapor above a blue haze of desert dust and heat. But later, from the back of a saddle horse on a chilly May morning, I found that the mountains were no floating illusion. My knees felt every step as the horse plodded up the trail that starts in the verdant Basin area and climbs to the South Rim of the Chisos. Even so there is a real enchantment here, beginning with the very name Chisos, which may have derived from either an Indian or a Spanish word for bewitched or ghostly. But mostly the enchantment lies in the lofty peaks themselves, rising so abruptly out of the hot, dry Chihuahuan Desert.

Our group of six riders climbed higher, looking back at the jutting volcanic formations below us, and up at massive Casa Grande looming above. We wound through lush grass in Laguna Meadows, then through forests of maples, oaks, cypresses, and aspens. Trail guide David Alloway regaled us with lore of the area. At the South Rim only a few scrubby pines dotted the open escarpment. Two thousand feet below spread the desert floor, broken here and there by formations like the Elephant Tusk and the Mule Ears. "About 400 feet to the first bounce," said Dave cheerily. At a distance we could see Castolon Peak near where the Rio Grande breaks through Santa Elena Canyon. Farther away, into Mexico, rose high palisades and towering peaks. "I don't know how many times I get up here," Dave said, "but I never get tired of it."

Later, with Park Service staff members Tom and Betty Alex, I drove many miles in the park, across scrubby Chihuahuan terrain, where outcroppings of volcanic dikes and plugs protruded jaggedly out of the eroded landscape. We passed remnants of stone and adobe houses and old windmills, tilted like huge, broken-winged birds, marking where ranches once were. In places, spindly lechuguilla and sotol poked up out of the brush like the spears of a thousand warriors lying in wait. Ocotillo flashed red blossoms on the tips of gangling, leafless limbs.

It is a harsh land for man or beast. After the conquistadors spurned the region, it was left pretty much to desperados and dropouts, raiding Indians, and a few ranchers and hardscrabblers trying to survive. Today people still drop out here, but, instead of evading the law, they are more apt to be forsaking city hassles for the quiet of a derelict mining town like Terlingua, or Lajitas—where, in 1986, a beer-drinking goat named Clay Henry was nearly elected mayor.

The nearer you get to the Rio Grande, the more Texas and Mexico seem to blend. Even the plants speak lilting Spanish—ocotillo, lechuguilla, cholla, candelilla—that belies their spiky natures. On both sides of the river, low, flat-roofed houses cling to the land. Isolated farm communities on the Mexican side—peaceful since the end of the bandit raids early in this century—often have more contact with Texas than with the rest of Mexico.

Before I left Big Bend, Tom and Betty took me to a place that is special to them. We drove over a rugged four-wheel-drive road and stopped at a stark, eroded formation called Ernst Tinaja. At first we walked past sinuous walls of white rock. "This is the Buda Limestone," said Tom. Wind and water had carved deep holes into the limestone, hence the name "tinaja," which is Spanish for basin or jar. They hold water year-round and attract wildlife. Deep claw marks gouged into the slick, steep sides of the largest of the water holes, Tom told me, show where, a few years ago, a mountain lion tried desperately to escape before it drowned.

Farther up the canyon we reached rock terraces layered like pastry, twisted and buckled into the most extraordinary shapes. A palette of pinks, oranges, purples, yellows, golds swirled at my feet and up the canyon walls. "This is the Boquillas Flagstone," said Tom. But I knew better. I'd found the old vaquero's rainbow waiting for the rain.

Two worlds meet in the Chisos Mountains in the Big Bend country of west Texas. In the higher reaches of the Chisos lie lush meadows and hardwood forests more characteristic of cooler, wetter climes to the north. A symbol of the Chihuahuan Desert, dagger-spiked agave, foreground, wards off any intimate contact. Also called the century plant, the agave may spend 50 years storing energy to send up a single stalk a dozen feet tall, for one spectacular display of golden blossoms. Afterward, the plant withers and dies.

Dwarfed by the expanse of the Big Bend, a rider looks to Mexico from the Chisos Mountains. This isolated region offers visitors open spaces where such beauties as the claret cup cactus (opposite) grow—and blue skies that inspired one old-timer to claim: "When your lungs are full of Big Bend air, you seem to forget that you are gettin' older."

157

ontented grin lights the face of Lance Lacy atop his horse, Shorty. At his family's ranch near Fort Davis, the 11-year-old Texan lives every boy's dream—to be a real cowboy. "I like riding horses and working cattle and helping my dad!" His lasso awhirl, he aims for a calf during the spring roundup. Horses from the remuda, which provides mounts for the working cowhands, trot across dry Limpia Creek on the sprawling "06," one of the oldest ranches in the region. Behind rise volcanic formations typical of the Davis Mountains area. Each spring and fall, the whole Lacy family and their hands live out on the range for several weeks at a time, continuing a way of life that has gone on in these mountains since the 1850s.

Autumn ablaze in McKittrick Canyon shows why some call this small gorge in the Guadalupe Mountains the most beautiful spot in Texas. Such corners in the arid Southwest offer a special haven. At the edge of the windswept Chihuahuan Desert, this well-watered oasis shelters groves of maple, oak, and walnut. Ever moving on the wind, silken dunes of gypsum sand (pages 160-161) flow toward the massive western ramparts of the Guadalupes.

TOM ALGIRE

163

THE FAR WEST

Along the Continent's Restless Rim

Born of fire and shaped by erosion, the Far West showcases an epic geologic
conflict. Nature continues fashioning landscapes here—from California's
majestic Sierra Nevada to the surf-battered Washington coast, from
Alaska's glacial peaks to the green volcanic isles of Hawaii. A violent
upthrust of granite created El Capitan (opposite) in Yosemite National Park; Ice
Age glaciers gouged away softer surrounding rock. The glow of an oak's autumn
foliage (above) signals the changing seasons in Yosemite. Nearby, Yosemite Falls
(pages 166-167) plunges 2,425 feet; in the foreground bloom cow parsnips.

THE FAR WEST

By William Howarth
Photographs by
Richard Alexander
Cooke III

Scenic treasures of
Yosemite inspired Congress
in 1890 to designate it the
nation's second national
park, after Yellowstone.
To the north, the coast of
Washington endures as
one of America's last wild
shores—a place of lush
rain forests, protected
estuaries, and rocky cliffs.
In southeastern Alaska,
Misty Fiords National
Monument harbors a maze
of waterways towered over
by ice-wreathed peaks.
Far to the west, Molokai's
Kamakou Preserve shields
remnants of Hawaii's
native flora and fauna.

By noon the sleet is falling fast, swept by wind off the Sierra and pelting me with an icy rattle. I am wet, chilled to the bone and beginning to shudder, an early sign of hypothermia. But the horses and the mule are warm, even steaming, and up ahead Randy Potter looks dry in his bright yellow slicker and broad-brimmed hat. When I draw near, he pulls a long white sock from his saddlebag. "Try some of this. It's *way* good."

Randy is tall and rawboned, a redhead with quiet manners and a shy grin. By now I've learned that "way good" is his supreme praise, reserved mostly for country music and Liz, a friend at college. In summer he works as a wrangler in Yosemite National Park, packing mule trains up the long mountain trails. He also leads overnight saddle trips, sometimes for dudes who don't expect to freeze in California.

In the sock is a pint of apricot brandy. It's no cure for my shakes, but the sweet warmth spreads quickly and begins to lull my brain. A pint of sunlight . . . pale golden orange. Only yesterday, I had walked barefoot along a Pacific beach, watching sunset and the waves polish sand into bright, reflected gold. Then I left sea level and drove east for three hours, gaining 8,000 feet of elevation. Randy and I have climbed to 9,600 feet, where the sleet now swirls as snow, lifted by updrafts and drifted upon blooming asters. We are in the Sierra Nevada, Spanish for snowy mountain range. Today winter has arrived on September 3.

I've come to the highlands of Yosemite to begin a journey through the Far West, from California to the coast of Washington State, then to the fiords of lower Alaska and a tropical rain forest in Hawaii. I'm making a broad arc along the western rim of America, across country that seems young and edgy, restless with its own borders. Out here the land often heaves and seethes, buckled by earthquakes and volcanic eruptions. Rains wash the earth to sea, where waves beat and shape new shores. I've reached the physical limits of America, but that far boundary is not fixed and final.

My trip in Yosemite began at Tuolumne Meadows, and so far Randy and I have met only two other travelers—both outbound. We are riding up Lyell Canyon along the John Muir Trail. Little has changed here since the 1870s, when John Muir came to the region to tend sheep and run a sawmill. A brisk, bearded Scot with a passion for hiking, he spent his free time up in the mountains. For several years he explored the Sierra on foot, mapping remote areas and writing journal notes by firelight. He carried a pair of blankets, lived on bread and pots of black tea. Up here, he wrote, "[I] get as near the heart of the world as I can."

Often the horses' hooves clack and ring, as we pick a way around granite boulders. The gouged and rounded rocks are signs of glaciation, a once-disputed theory that naturalist Muir verified by finding active glaciers in the High Sierra. Just 10,000 years ago—a moment in geological time—great rivers of glacial ice flowed here and carved the surface features. Ice entered narrow canyons and carved wide, U-shaped valleys; ice also sliced off sections of huge granite domes. As it departed, the ice

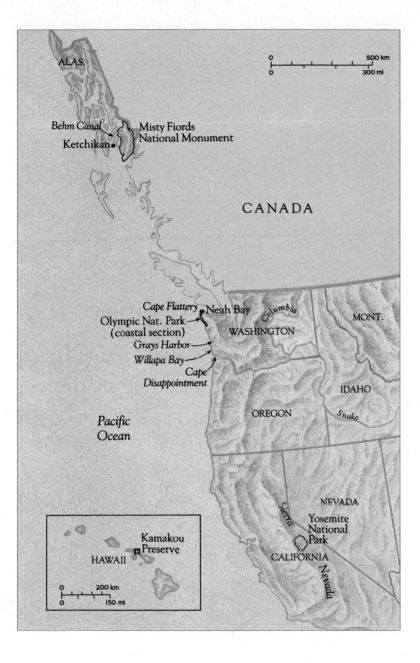

dumped its rocky till, these giant stones that await the next glacial cycle.

Cold and hungry, we reach tonight's destination at Vogelsang High Sierra Camp, a haven of tent cabins and *hot showers* at 10,200 feet. The camp is one of five maintained on a 50-mile loop trail, offering travelers a level of comfort that John Muir disdained. In the cookhouse, Paula Tisdale-Schremp is concocting tonight's supper of chili soup, salad, turkey with toasted rice, and hot apple pie. Small and trim, she works to the pulsing beat of a tape player. When she talks, her eyes and hands dance: "My regular job is sign-language interpreting for the deaf. This is my sixth summer in the Sierra. I keep saying it's the end, but. . . ." She turns to check the oven and reveals a T-shirt slogan: "Never Trust Anyone Under 10,000 Feet."

In the morning Paula takes me on a hike to some of her favorite Sierra scenes. We follow an alpine drainage, climbing from meadows to glassy pools, perfect mirrors for the snow peaks, then up past roaring cascades to a high, snow-fed lake known as Hanging Basket. It looks like an empty basket today, just a pool of dark water encircled by talus, the erosional debris from above. But some sharp, piercing barks greet us, and several brown snouts poke out of the rock piles. "Marmots," Paula says. "Look how fat they are."

Like their woodchuck and squirrel cousins, the marmots are storing fat for a long winter's sleep. They survive at this elevation by feeding mainly on alpine meadow grass, a lush but short-lived crop. Paula likes the marmots' air of bustle and self-importance. "Most of the year, they own this place. Every summer that bark is the first and last sound I hear, coming and going." She scoops up some fresh snow and takes a healthy bite. "And when I leave, the meadows are the color of marmot fur."

For two days Randy and I ride along the High Sierra loop trail, crossing what appear to be fields of living stone. In places the granite is so smooth, scraped and then polished by glacial action, that it lies flat and sun bleached, like a petrified prairie. Elsewhere the creeks and streams have etched deep, twisting ravines where patches of mist hang low and dim. The water that spills down these long-sloped shoulders seems to move over flowing liquid rock.

Randy names the Sierra trees for me: "Ponderosa pine, juniper, and that's lodgepole pine—the bark looks like a cracked window pane." In this thin soil and harsh climate the trees are all conifers, each with a different story of challenge and survival. We pass a fallen lodgepole, its silver grain twisted into tight barber-pole spirals. "Lightning-welded," Randy explains. "The bolt hit up high and then spun down." Nearby stands an untouched Jeffrey pine, spreading its open crown to a dry, sunny day. I crush a twig and smell its youthful aromas: fresh lemon, shading off to a twist of vanilla.

On our last full day together, Randy and I set off from Sunrise High Sierra Camp for a cross-country hike to see the Cathedral Range, a series of peaks that lie across the northern horizon. We start off briskly, then slow the pace while scaling steep ridges. "Now I know why I love horses," Randy mutters. "But we'd need a goat to climb here." The rock underfoot makes for hard walking, alternately smooth slopes and then piles of jagged rubble. Pressure and weathering cause the stone to exfoliate, cracking and peeling layers like skin from a boiled onion. During one of many stops, we exfoliate our jackets and rest.

Randy and I have traded stories and jokes, but now our talk turns serious. "Working up here has made a difference in my life," he says. "I never thought much about religion, but last summer I took a party of Mennonite people out for a three-day ride. One night we got to talking and they asked: 'Where do you worship?' 'Here,' I told them. 'What do you think of when you're away?' 'How soon I'm going to get back.' "

At the last ridge, we climb upward into waves of light and dark, as snow clouds sweep across the sun. With every step the wind grows stronger, rising from gusts to a steady gale. At the top Randy leans on the wind as it tears by with a freight-train roar. We look out upon a world of peaks, a skyline of mountain ranges that rise in abrupt cones, horn-shaped snags, and deep, swelling saddles. He points out the landmarks: "That's Matthes Crest, Cockscomb, and Unicorn. Over there is Cathedral; sort of looks like a big steeple."

"The Range of Light," Muir called his Sierra, and today light is racing by in swift flashes of glory, flying before the dark but enfolding it behind, flowing with the pulses that drive the wind. The highest snow-clad peaks flare like beacons, graced by the light, beyond the reach of all but our vision. Facing into the wind, Randy and I don't say much more. But turning to go, we both grin and say together, "*waaay* good."

Two days later I am some 600 miles north, at the lower tip of Washington State. From mountains I have descended to a shoreline famous in American history. Not far from here the Lewis and Clark expedition arrived on November 7, 1805, after 18 months spent crossing the western continent. In his journal Clark wrote: "Great joy . . . we are in *view* of the *Ocian* . . . this great Pacific Octean which we been so long anxious to See. and the roreing or noise made by the waves brakeing on the rockey Shores (as I suppose) may be heard disti[n]ctly. . . ."

Their joy was premature, for the explorers were in fact still on the Columbia River. Ten more days of travel passed before Lewis finally stood where I now stand. The beach is flat and sandy, ruffled by long waves of white-tipped combers. Out there lies a ship's graveyard, hundreds of wrecks lost to storms and shoals. A British sea captain named the place Cape Disappointment, but today it seems quite promising. All day I had driven through the dark, cold rain of early fall; now the sun has broken through to make a bright farewell. The scene is painted by light: It glistens on the green, nodding beach grass, adds a luster to the humped sand dunes and wet shoreline. This sand stretches far north of Cape Disappointment to form Long Beach peninsula, a mile wide and 28 miles long—one of the world's longest beaches . . . for now.

Sand is a fickle substance, the end product of erosion, endlessly shifted by wind and waves. This barrier beach formed just a few thousand years ago, and a major storm could breach it overnight. But not on this fair evening. Nearby a glaucous-winged gull rests on the sand, watching raincoated folk take their twilight strolls.

As the sun drops and colors deepen, people become black shadows reflected in the tidal pools. The beach turns into a burnished mirror, with clouds billowing impossibly in the dark sand, and two suns, above and below, rushing to meet each other. Now the sand is molten,

Startling in brilliance, snow plant blossoms herald the approach of spring at trailside in Yosemite Valley. This member of the wintergreen family lives on decaying vegetation and sometimes pushes through snow to bloom. PAGES 174-175: Visitors traverse rocky switchbacks at the base of 320-foot-high Vernal Fall. Windblown curtains of moisture torn from the thick wall of water prompted the name of the hikers' route: the Mist Trail.

brighter than an explorer's dreams of western gold. The sun flares and fades, and into this scene comes a young traveler, Chinese, pedaling a fat-tired bike. He makes his way slowly along the rose and blue pools, bike wheels reflected as constant figure eights.

For several days I drive north along the coast, following the deep curves of Willapa Bay and Grays Harbor. Protected from the sea, shorelines change from sand to mud flats. The flats are estuarial, built by deposits from river currents and drained by ocean tides. In these briny wetlands, life prospers with a rich diversity. Mud is home to crab and shrimp, the burrowing clam and delectable oyster. This food draws herons, ducks, and other shorebirds to dwell in nearby marshes.

Summer's people have left the coast, just as the bird migrations begin. Down from the arctic waters fly Canada geese, brant, American wigeon, and loons; at Willapa National Wildlife Refuge and other protected areas, they feed on succulent grasses. Thousands of them cover the bays, diving or dabbling for food, huddled in flocks to rest and ride out storms. They also populate the shuttered resort towns: At Ocean Shores, birds are nesting on Scoter Drive and Tern Place.

North of Grays Harbor, I see a gradual change come to beaches on the Olympic Peninsula. For 25 miles the sand is broad and hard-packed, firm enough to support cars. At Pacific Beach I join the two-way traffic posted "25 mph, No Squirreling." That means no zigzagging, especially near the waterline, where beds of young clams lie beneath the sand. But a rocky shoreline emerges at the Quinault River, and there driving halts. Ahead lies the coastal section of Olympic National Park and stretches of Native American tribal lands. This expanse forms the great wilderness beach of Washington, 80 miles accessible mainly by foot.

For a few hours I shoulder a light pack and hike along one of America's last wild shores. To make an overnight journey, I would need stout gear and good tide tables. The trail winds along narrow beach strips, much of it passable only at low tide. Often I must climb a steep bluff to ford creeks or bypass headland capes. Soon wind and rain are adding to the fun, along with a skunk that tries to mooch my dinner. Yet I am not the only tourist out here. At the trailhead on Kalaloch Creek I meet two hikers with giant backpacks. Their names? "Just say Mike and Mary, from Seattle." Barefoot and in rolled-up pants, they are wet but happy. "The tent blew down twice last night, but today we saw whales!"

On the Kalaloch beach, weathered rocks rise up to meet the waves. The surf rolls in on long, curling breakers, five or six to a set. Wind sweeps the waves ashore until they topple, then recede. The sea's energy here is prodigious: It strikes each square foot of beach with as much as two tons of pressure, enough to uproot trees and strip them naked, to pile up acres of driftwood and twisted kelp. Waves also erode away the land, isolating "sea stacks" of rock that lie offshore, like haystacks marooned in a flood. One tiny stack stands at the water's edge, waving a single tree. Returning to my car, I pass through the park's famed Hoh rain forest. Almost on cue, a cool (Continued on page 186)

Sunlight filters through hemlocks and western red cedars on Long Island in Willapa National Wildlife Refuge on the Washington coast. This stand shelters a remnant of the lowland maritime forests once common along our northwestern shores. In Olympic National Park, fern fiddleheads (below) uncurl toward the light. PAGES 178-179: Attesting the power of Pacific surf and storms, wave-curved sea stacks stand sentinel near the park's Sitka spruce-clad coast.

B right chain of tidal pools reflects the morning sky at Shi Shi Beach in the coastal section of Washington's Olympic National Park. Such pools shelter a variety of plant and animal life. At the bottom of the pools live barnacles, limpets, periwinkles, and mussels. An abnormally low tide has stranded a clump of starfish (below). PAGES 182-183: Hardy Sitka spruce—resistant to wind and salt spray—forest the top of a sea stack looming out of the mist.

PAT O'HARA (BOTH)

BRONWYN COOKE

ROBERT J. WESTERN

184

More than head high, fronds of hāpu'u, or tree fern, crown
the rim of Waikolu Valley in the Kamakou Preserve on the
Hawaiian Island of Molokai. Ranging from arid shrubland to
summit rain forest, the preserve's varied habitats contain more than 250
species of plants—219 of them found only in Hawaii. Opposite, lower,
an 'i'iwi, a rare honeycreeper, feeds on nectar from blossoms of the
koli'i plant. 'Ōhi'a-lehua flowers (opposite) burst forth year-round.

rain descends. The trees here receive so much water, 80 to 90 inches a year, that every surface teems with green, bearded mosses and sprays of fern. Cycles of life and death quicken, blurring together. Seedlings arise from nurse logs, the bodies of fallen parents. Uprooted trees expose dense, abstract tangles of root, where birds peck for insects. The dim forest produces misshapen trees with horned branches and swollen burls, draped with fat banana slugs. When showers end, a steamy vapor rises—to descend before long as another rain.

I catch some final glimpses of the sea's power at La Push, a beach heaped with wave-smoothed cobblestones. As surf rushes in and out, the stones answer with a rattling chorus, gleaming wetly in hues of ebony and pearl. Just beyond lies Cape Flattery, the most northwesterly point in the lower 48 states. Here a trail leads through Sitka spruce and elderberry bushes to the edge of sheer cliffs. Two hundred feet below, waves have carved deep caves and fluted pillars in the high rock walls. No safety rails here, so another visitor has strapped her son on her back, papoose-style. He gives me a solemn wave.

In two days I have crossed four Indian reservations, those of the Quinault, Quileute, Hoh, and Makah. At the time of Lewis and Clark, these people were masters at using the forest and sea. In those days they hunted whales from cedar canoes and lived in cedar slab houses. Today the Makah settlement at Neah Bay is a modern town in all respects, but its native culture remains strong and proud. In the gleaming two-million-dollar Makah Cultural and Research Center, I talk with director Greig Arnold about local conditions.

"Like in many small towns, unemployment remains our biggest problem, but not groceries. When the tide goes out, the refrigerator door is open—you can find any seafood you like." Greig's job is to help preserve the Makah heritage, through public education and museum displays. "We say that Makah have lived here from the beginning of time. And we intend to stay. This center is our heritage school, with classes in carving, weaving, painting, and the Makah language."

From American University in Washington, D.C., Ann Renker came to this western Washington town to learn Makah—and wound up directing the language program. "Mainly we teach children, who are teaching their parents. Makah nearly died out a generation ago. Only ten native speakers survive." Makah had no functional alphabet until 1979; now a growing library records the tribal tales and history.

"In spring, we take children to the shore and have them hunt for"—she makes some clicking, guttural sounds: Makah for starfish, whelk, and sea urchin. Ann has focused part of her own research on how the language describes nature. "You greet people according to the skies. And every plant and animal has an exact, ranked name." Bristling with energy, Ann learned restraint to gain the trust of elders. About to resume her doctoral studies, she departs with a tribal name, *Oo-sid-ee*. "In my early days, they'd see me running and call 'hurry up, hurry up.'"

Another 600-mile leap northward, to the lower tip of the Alaska

Panhandle, brings me to Misty Fiords National Monument, a world of steep mountains and mazy waterways, where glaciers sprawl above vast domains of untracked forest. My first impression is of fresh, clean air washed by a million rains. The journey begins in Ketchikan, one of the wettest towns in North America.

Rain falls steadily on this seaward edge of Revillagigedo Island, more than 150 inches a year. People live in rain gear, going about their jobs in bright blue and yellow slickers. Under dark, roiled skies they slosh through puddles of "liquid sunshine," never fearing a drought. Water lies everywhere: It rains upon the hills and pours into streams that swell Ketchikan Creek, a torrent that rushes through town to the sea.

Against this flow leap the dark bodies of salmon, heading upstream in their last rite of life. As they make the spawning journey from salt to fresh water, some fish are captured by hatcheries for artificial breeding. But many reach the shallows of cold, fast-running streams. For an hour one morning I sit by the rapids of Ketchikan Creek to watch dozens of king salmon. In this fresh water they no longer feed, and their bodies are turning blood-red. They hang motionless in the current, a squadron of thin, dark torpedoes bent on one final mission.

Salmon gave new life to Ketchikan after the gold rush days of the 1890s. A dozen canneries operated in the area in the early 1900s, processing fish caught by a fleet of private boats. The fishermen went upstream as well, going up Creek Street to visit the "girls" who took in trade of the ill-famed kind. They lived in houses built on pilings above Ketchikan Creek; today the old red-light district sports gift shops and cafes for the cruise boat trade. At Dolly Arthur's house, the tour guide is a freckled 15; wearing braces, she lisps the word "prostitution."

Dolly's house is a totem of sorts, a reminder of earlier days and legends. A host of Native American totems stands in Saxman, a Tlingit village southeast of Ketchikan. From abandoned towns and cemeteries the Tlingit have gathered many carved cedar poles, the tribe's silent storytellers. In morning mist the totems face out to sea, a company of ravens with jutting beaks, beavers that clutch sticks, owl-face masks with eyes protruding. Many symbolize heroic figures that fly and swim forever. Cedar has its own powers: One pole has sprouted some new green shoots.

From Ketchikan, I head northeast for an aerial survey of Misty Fiords National Monument. This 4,062-square-mile region, nearly twice the size of Delaware, is a prime example of wild, roadless Alaskan bush. My pilot is Royle Snodderly, a veteran of ten years of flying in all kinds of weather. As we pass over Behm Canal, the hundred-mile ocean inlet reaching into Misty Fiords, he looks down at flat, black water: "Winter time, the wind blows 65 knots. We get nasty waves down there—and horizontal rain." All year he carries mail and supplies to outlying towns; on clear days, paying passengers—"flight-seers"—come along to marvel at Misty Fiords. As Royle banks and turns the plane, we cross steep granite cliffs mantled with snow, then sweep over wide U-shaped valleys and rough-rimmed cirques, totems left by the carving ice. We pass hanging lakes, with long plumes of cascading outlet streams, then fly up the Chickamin River, its water a milky olive-green. "Glacial melt," Royle says. "More silt than water."

We spot several mountain goats as the plane climbs, rising from snow ridges to packed fields of ice. "It's always winter up here," Royle notes, as we approach 8,000 feet and the massive white crown of Soulé Glacier. On a closer pass I see that the Soulé has a dark, wrinkled surface, like skin dusted with soot. The ice glows a faint pastel blue, with surface contour lines. "Those are flow lines," says Royle, "like currents in a river."

A day later I'm chugging up Behm Canal with Malcolm Doiron, a fishing guide who doubles as a carpenter. A life spent outdoors has made him into an ardent conservationist. "In the late 1960s and '70s several of us worked hard to make this place a national monument. We drew up the boundaries on a map. Then sitting at a kitchen table one night we came up with a name, Misty Fiords." The idea had its opponents in Ketchikan, he recalls, those who feared excessive regulations: "The air services fought us the most, but today they're making the tourist money."

From a plane I had *seen* the Misty Fiords; in Malcolm's boat, I begin to feel them. For two days we make a slow journey along the canal, pausing to picnic on islands or going ashore to fish in streams. Several trails lead to lakes, where cabins await fly-in campers. "We'll have to keep an eye out for brown bears," Malcolm says. "This is good fishing territory for them, too." In the evening we camp at Punchbowl Cove off the main channel, moored below 3,000-foot cliffs. Water slaps softly on the boat's sides; two seals play near our stern. As shadows rise up the steep stone walls, Malcolm smiles with contentment. "This place is the Yosemite of Alaska."

Later, I explore more distant waters on an excursion boat skippered by Dale Pihlman from Ketchikan. One of his passengers today is the exuberant Tommie Lee de Armas. Cuban-born and now from St. Louis, she marvels at the ice-bound vistas: "With scenery like this, who wants to go home?" In Walker Cove, we nose our way up to a waterfall, fill a pitcher with snowmelt and toast the crew's health. On another cliff appear two large white rings, near the waterline: ancient petroglyphs? "No," Dale says. "Those were big lichen colonies, now washed away."

A native Alaskan, Dale has worked as a teacher, marine biologist, fisherman, and now tour boat captain. He likes the rigors of this country, as only a native can: "I love rough weather. The fishing is best when everyone else is in harbor." As we begin our return to Ketchikan, mist descends the fiord slopes. The seawater in Behm Canal is calm and flat; we thread our way among islands and finally reach Ketchikan, long after dark. Dale checks the clear, starry sky. "No rain tonight . . . but I won't bet on tomorrow."

One last jump—2,500 miles westward, beyond the mainland—brings me to Kamakou, a tropical forest preserve on the Hawaiian Island of Molokai. Small in size and population, Molokai has no traffic jams or high-rise hotels—and this quiet pace may be its best attraction. At a gas station I ask a young woman for directions to Kaunakakai, the island center: "You go down to 'da corner, turn lef', an'a whole town is dere." The main street is one block long, crammed with grocery stores.

For years Molokai was a truck garden for Hawaii, mainly given to raising beef and pineapples on its western plateau. The famous leper colony of Kalaupapa, now a national historical park, sits on the remote northern shore, isolated by 4,000-foot sea cliffs. For a small island, Molokai holds much of Hawaii's best: powdery sand, exported to build Waikiki Beach in Honolulu; one of the earliest sites of human dwellings; and one of the largest stands of rare native plants. Legends say that Molokai also inspired the hula—in which bodies flutter like windblown leaves of an 'ōlapa tree.

Better hang on," Ed Misaki grins. "It gets a little bumpy here." Manager of the Kamakou Preserve, Ed is putting his four-wheeler through its own hula lessons. As we roar up a swampy, rutted jungle trail, the car heads *mauka,* inland, but often we are b-bouncing *makai,* seaward. Those are Hawaii's two compass directions. Volcanic eruptions built these islands into mountainous masses that slope to the coasts. "You can also tell that Molokai is volcanic," Ed says, "from its rough topography and iron-rich soil."

Ed is a Hawaiian-born Japanese, a biologist who once dreamed of playing pro baseball. Still in top shape, he takes the lead as we begin to hike up Papaala Pali, the summit ridge of Molokai. "We're going to nearly 5,000 feet, so you'll see some big changes in habitat," he promises. Soon we have passed from dry slopes to a cool, dim rain forest, lush with vegetation. We are climbing back into Molokai's past, a botanical Eden. "Up here the plants are 90 percent endemic," Ed says. "They grew only in Hawaii until man arrived." Then came settlement—and the long, slow fall of paradise.

"The native plants had no thorns or poisonous sap because there were no predators. When people put in crops and let livestock loose, the native foliage was often trampled, eaten, or crowded out." We pause at Waikolu Valley overlook, a break in the jungle that opens to a view of dry, scrubby plains. "Once most of eastern Molokai was rain forest," Ed says, "but now only 30 percent of the forest is left."

The best of that remaining forest lies within the Kamakou Preserve, which Ed manages for the Nature Conservancy of Hawaii. Within this mountain and valley wilderness live hundreds of endemic plants, birds, and insects, a riot of fertile growth. But Ed is guarding a delicate system: "An island is so isolated that its species are unique, highly specialized.

They can't compete with heavy stress—and when you lose a species here, it's gone for good."

After a lunch of hamburger and sushi, we move along a cleated boardwalk through a mountain bog, Pepeopae. Amid mosses and sedges, the *'ōhi'a-lehua* tree thrives, but not to its usual height of 60 feet. "Bog soil is wet and acidic, so all the trees are stunted." Ed stoops beside some natural bonsai, ten-inch 'ōhi'as with full red blooms. Looking up, he sees another flash of scarlet: " *'Apapane*—it drinks the 'ōhi'a nectar with a long, curved beak." Two of Hawaii's rarest birds live up here, the *oloma'o* and the *kakawahie,* a thrush and a honeycreeper that are both endangered species.

At our highest overlook we will see the northern pali coast and its great sea cliffs, but reaching that spot, barely 800 feet above the bog, takes an hour of sloshing along a wet jungle trail. "Kamakou is like a big sponge," Ed says, "always absorbing and releasing moisture." "Moist" is not my word for this quagmire, I think, as we cross muddy sloughs that pull at our boots with a loud sucking noise. But the water also yields bright clusters of orchids and woody violets, silver lilies and giant tree ferns. Ed touches some *maile* vines. "In old times, this was the best lei to give—not for showy flowers, but the sweet, milky smell."

One last turn, and we step to the edge of old times. Beneath us the Pelekunu Valley drops away, a dizzying fall of 3,000 feet into a broad, green bowl of jungle. A strong wind is lifting patches of mist up and over the ridge. These prevailing trade winds soak the valley with almost daily rain. My eye traces several long, thin plumes of waterfall that pitch downward, pausing at plunge pools to regather force, then rushing on to the sea. "Down there are ruins of dwellings built by early Hawaiians," Ed says. The first Hawaiians came here from the south of Polynesia, possibly to escape wars and overcrowding.

Two days later I'm still thinking of those explorers as Clifford Soares takes me on a farewell helicopter flight over the island. In lilting English, Portuguese-accented with Hawaiian slang, he talks of his own pioneer days on Molokai. "I made a botanical survey of the Pelekunu Valley and lived there four years. We put up a tent house and raised three kids. My wife and I taught the school lessons; I hiked out for supplies and mail." Was the family lonely? "No, being up there is best."

As Clifford flies a long, winding circle around Molokai, my thoughts are turning on those words. Being there—experiencing a place for the first time—is the dream of every traveler. The Polynesians came north to find Hawaii. The great dream of Europeans was to follow the sun to new lands. So many journeys America's pioneering travelers made: A ship rounding Cape Cod . . . trekking the dark Cumberland Gap . . . Lake Superior, via canoe . . . over the Rockies and across the southwestern deserts . . . standing at last on the wide Pacific shore.

"To what end does the world go on," mused Henry Thoreau, "and why was America discovered?" Perhaps to spark forever the love of exploration, in a nation still drawn to the beauty of this radiant land.

River of ice on its way to the sea, Through Glacier grinds down a valley in Misty Fiords National Monument amid mountains of the Coast Range of southeastern Alaska. In the distance, Chickamin Glacier clings to snow-dusted Mount Jefferson Coolidge. Eons of volcanism and glaciation combined with a rising sea level to create the monument's awesome landscape. Here mighty peaks tower above a coastline indented by narrow fiords and flanked by islands of dense forest.

reezes ripple the reflection of steep valley walls at the head of Walker Cove in Misty Fiords National Monument. Conifers cling to pockets of earth, maintaining precarious footholds. Within the monument's more than 4,000 square miles lie environments ranging from impenetrable alder thickets to alpine valleys to mountaintops perpetually clad in ice. More than 150 inches of rain and snow fall here each year. At times clouds dip low, shrouding the fiords. PAGES 194-195: Mists swirling about a threadlike waterfall offer one final window on America.

Notes on Contributors

Free-lance photographer JOSÉ AZEL was born in Cuba and moved to the U.S. at age eight. A graduate of Cornell and the University of Missouri, José has contributed to TRAVELER and other U.S. and European magazines. This is his first major assignment for Special Publications.

Hawaii-born photographer RICHARD ALEXANDER COOKE III holds degrees from UCLA and the University of Oregon. He has had varied free-lance assignments for the Society, including chapters in *Canada's Wilderness Lands* and *Builders of the Ancient World*.

A resident of Louisville, free lance DAN DRY was named the National Press Photographers Association Newspaper Photographer of the Year in 1981. A frequent contributor to the Society, Dan photographed a chapter in the Special Publication *America's Hidden Corners*.

Free-lance photographer DAVID HISER recently completed his 50th assignment for the Society. The subjects he has covered range from Aztecs to polar bears. Among the numerous books that his work has appeared in are *Splendors of the Past*, *Trails West*, and *Blue Horizons*.

Free-lance writer WILLIAM HOWARTH has contributed to *America's Wild Woodlands* and *Great Rivers of the World*. He has also written four articles for NATIONAL GEOGRAPHIC. Bill is writing the Special Publication *Traveling the Trans-Canada*, to be published in December 1987.

Senior writer CHRISTINE ECKSTROM LEE joined the Society staff in 1974. The coauthor of *America's Atlantic Isles*, she has written chapters for numerous other Special Publications, including *Our Awesome Earth*, *Exploring America's Valleys*, and *Blue Horizons*.

Free lance MARK MILLER has worked in print and broadcast journalism. He has contributed articles to NATIONAL GEOGRAPHIC and has written two chapters for the Special Publication *America's Spectacular Northwest*. Mark lives in Los Angeles, where he works as a screenwriter.

Senior writer THOMAS O'NEILL has been a Society staff member since 1976. He has written on subjects ranging from Pompeii to the Canadian wilderness. Tom is the author of *Back Roads America* and *Lakes, Peaks, and Prairies: Discovering the United States-Canadian Border*.

Writer BILL RICHARDS has free-lanced frequently for Society publications. His contributions include articles for NATIONAL GEOGRAPHIC, TRAVELER, and WORLD magazines, and two chapters in the Special Publication *America's Spectacular Northwest*. Bill lives in Chicago.

Before turning to free-lance photography, San Francisco-based PHILIP SCHERMEISTER was a news photographer for the Topeka *Capital-Journal*. Phil has contributed several stories to WORLD magazine. This is his first major assignment for Special Publications.

Senior writer JENNIFER C. URQUHART joined the Society staff in 1971. She has written chapters for several Special Publications, including *America's Great Hideaways*, *America's Wild Woodlands*, and *America's Wild and Scenic Rivers*. Jenny has also contributed to TRAVELER.

Tufts of snakeweed dot the bank of the Green River in Utah's Canyonlands National Park. River perspectives and cliff-top views give visitors here a lasting impression of America's natural beauty.

Acknowledgments

The Special Publications Division is grateful to the organizations and individuals named or quoted in the text and to those cited here for their assistance in the preparation of this book: G. Franklin Ackerman, Chris and Paula Andress, Ken Benad, Karen Berggren, Herman Channel, Charlie Crail, Wilson Francis, Jim Hidy, Alan Holt, Randy Jones, Bob Latham, Clenton Owensby, Steve Pardue, Sharon Raye, Jim Traub, Mark A. Wight, Mary Williams, Yosemite National Park Research Library.

Additional Reading

Readers may consult the *National Geographic Index* for related books and articles and refer to the following publications: Bruce Babbit, *Grand Canyon: An Anthology*; Jim Bones, Jr., *Texas West of the Pecos*; Sherwin Carlquist, *Hawaii, A Natural History*; C. Gregory Crampton, *Standing Up Country*; William Donohue Ellis, *Land of the Inland Seas*; Paul Friggens, *Gold and Grass: The Black Hills Story*; Aubrey Haines, *The Yellowstone Story*; Robert L. Kincaid, *The Wilderness Road*; Stephen Kulik, et al, *The Audubon Society Field Guide to Natural Places of the Northeast*; Charles McCarry, *The Great Southwest*; John Madson, *Where the Sky Began*; Ged Petit, "Reelfoot," in *Tennessee Wildlife*, January/February 1984; Gloria Snively, *Exploring the Seashore in British Columbia, Washington and Oregon*; Freeman Tilden, *The National Parks*.

INDEX

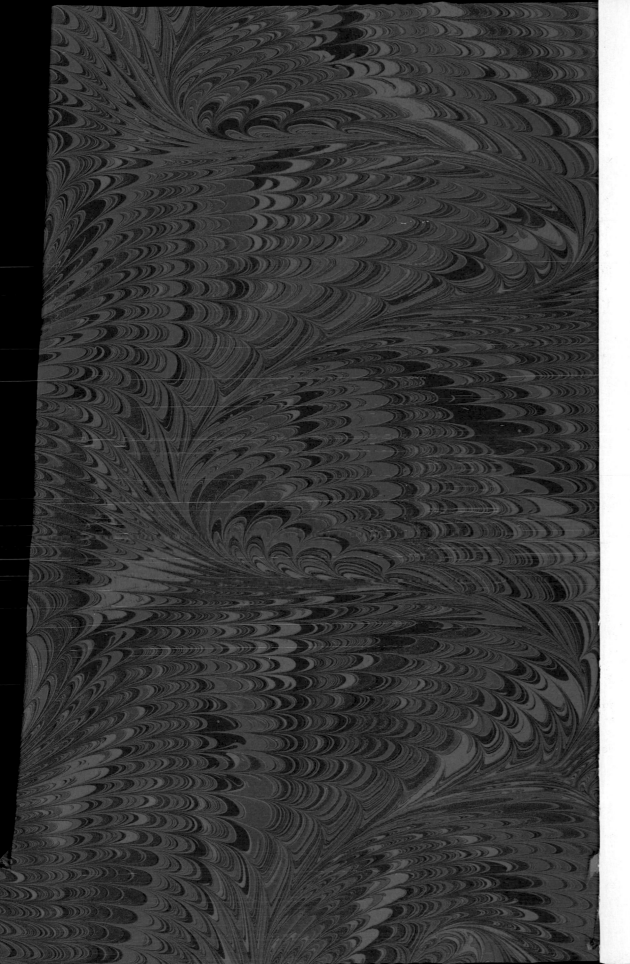

Library of Congress CIP Data
Window on America.
  Bibliography: p.
  Includes index.
    1. United States—Description and travel—1981-   2. United States—Description and travel—1981-   —Views.   3. Natural history—United States.   4. Natural history—United States—Pictorial works.   I. National Geographic Society (U. S.)
E169.04.W56   1987   917.3   86-33209
ISBN 0-87044-588-X (regular edition)   ISBN 0-87044-593-6 (library edition)

Composition for *Window on America* by National Geographic's Photographic Services, Carl M. Shrader, Director, Lawrence F. Ludwig, Assistant Director. Printed and bound by Holladay-Tyler Printing Corp., Rockville, Md. Film preparation by Catherine Cooke Studio, Inc., New York, N.Y. Color separations by Lanman Progressive Company, Washington, D.C.; Lincoln Graphics, Inc., Cherry Hill, N.J.; and NEC, Inc., Nashville, Tenn. Endpapers by Pamela S. Smith, Marblesmith Paper, Santa Fe, N.M.

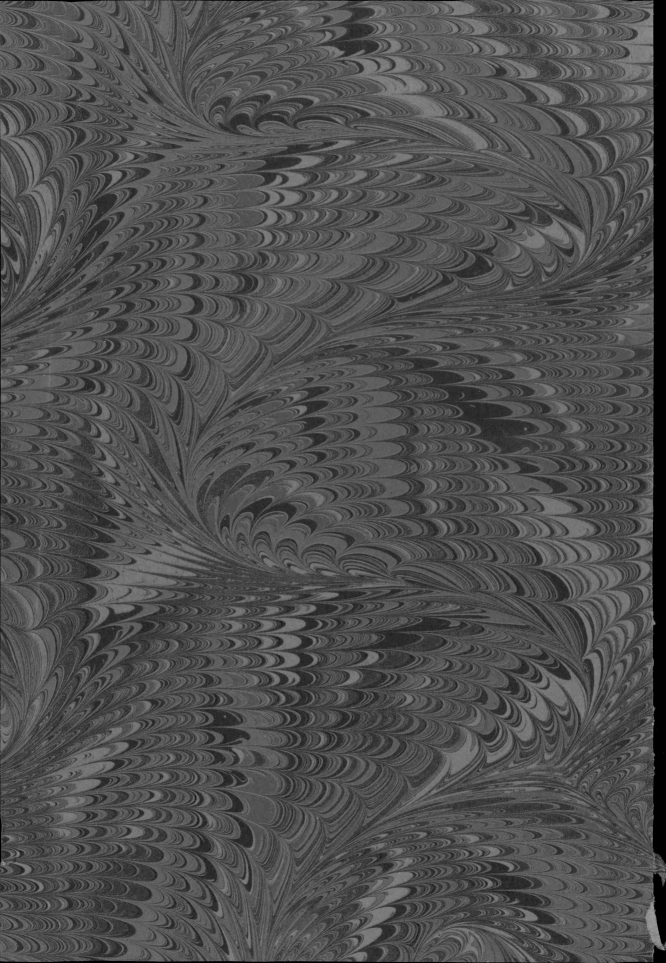